Ex libris

The
Celtic Image

The Celtic Image

Courtney Davis and David James

BLANDFORD

First published in Paperback 1997 in the UK by
BLANDFORD
A Cassell imprint
Wellington House
125 Strand
London WC2R 0BB

Previously Published in Hardback 1996

Distributed in the United States by Sterling Publishing Co., Inc.
387 Park Avenue South, New York, NY 10016-8810

**A Cataloguing-in-Publication Data entry for this title is available
from the British Library**

ISBN-0-7137-2482-x

Designed by Richard Carr
Printed and bound in Hong Kong by Dah Hua

Contents

Dedicated to the Celtic Spirit and the artists and craftsmen whose work inspired this Bøk.

Introduction

Like a sparkling crystal, the image of the Celt has many beautiful and varied facets. In this book it is our intention to touch on the various aspects, from the earliest known origins through to the present day. In order to do this, a brief historical perspective is necessary.

The earliest recorded Celtic civilization dates from around 700 BC. These people, known as Keltoi by early classical writers, lived in tribal and nomadic communities, frequently engaging in territorial warfare with their neighbours. Hallstatt, a large prehistoric salt-mining area in Austria, was their main territory in the seventh and sixth centuries BC.

Throughout the fifth century BC the La Tène area became a focus for the Celts, La Tène being a Swiss lakeside settlement on Lake Neuchâtel. The fine metalwork of this era is well known.

Venturing further afield in the fourth century BC, the Celts settled in northern Italy, invading Rome around 390 BC. Their itinerant and warfaring nature took them as far as Greece, where an invasion of Delphi is recorded in 279 BC. Soon after this, a group of Celts travelled even further into Galatia and subsequently settled there.

During the second century BC, Roman military forces increased in strength. First southern France and subsequently the whole of Gaul was conquered by Julius Caesar's army. The Celts were now forced to travel even further north.

It was during this era that many Celts arrived in Britain. From the second century BC onwards, they are known to have established tribal communities throughout Britain: about thirty-three of these are historically recorded.

Yet it is also possible that as early as 2000 BC communities with Celtic origins already existed in both Britain and Ireland, and were slowly joined and enlarged by traders and nomadic warriors from Europe.

A major tin-trading route from Asia Minor to Cornwall, the Phoenician Trading Route, had been in existence since the first millennium BC and almost certainly some Celtic migrants came to Britain in this way. At one time, Cornwall was the largest tin-producing country in the Western world.

From AD 43 Britain came permanently under Roman occupation and the majority of Celtic tribes were disbanded. Survivors amalgamated with the Anglo-Saxon kingdoms that were created after the invasions from about 500 AD onwards.

The relatively safer havens of what are now known as the Celtic countries – Cornwall, Wales, Ireland, Scotland, the Isle of Man and Brittany – remained. Despite fierce Viking invasions of all these areas, mainly during the ninth and tenth centuries AD, the Celtic spirit has remained alive, and these countries are now the present-day focus for the revival of Celtic culture.

Ireland, being more remote and thus relatively undisturbed, became the cornerstone of Celtic Christianity from the fourth century AD onwards. Just how the original Christian monks reached Ireland is not known, but again the Phoenician Trading Route is a strong possibility. It is said that Joseph of Arimathea travelled to Britain in this manner and established the first Celtic Christian church in Glastonbury in the first century AD. Voyages from the West Country to Ireland would have been a relatively simple matter for these hardy, seafaring monks.

Masterpieces of Celtic art such as the Books of Durrow and Armagh were created in Ireland in the period spanning the sixth to eighth centuries AD and many of the illustrious seafaring Celtic monks who ended up in Cornwall, Wales, Scotland and Brittany were either Irish themselves or of Irish descent. A notable example was the Irish-born St Columba, who founded the monastic settlement on Iona in 563 AD. The Book of Kells is said to have been created by Irish monks on this island.

In all of the present-day Celtic countries there are examples of prehistoric stone circles, standing stones and burial cairns. It should be made clear that these are not Celtic *per se*, as they were already in existence many hundreds of years before the arrival of the Celts. However, a thread of continuity is to be found, as many of these ancient sites were used by the Celtic people and subsequently by the early Celtic Christians.

For example, St Non's sixth-century-AD chapel in south-west Dyfed, Wales, is built within a prehistoric stone circle. Likewise, the present church at Ysbyty Cynfyn, near Devil's Bridge in Dyfed, also stands within a stone circle. There are further examples in other Celtic countries of burial chambers and standing stones linked with early chapels or churches still in use today. Some standing stones have a Christian cross carved on them and earlier ones have ogham inscriptions. Ogham script originated in Ireland and was the first written 'alpha-bet' used by the Celts. The inscriptions on these stones date from between the third and fifth centuries AD. It is also interesting to note that the original Scots Gaelic for 'going to church', when translated, is 'going to the stones'.

The cumdach *or book-shrine of Missel Stowe, Clonmacnoise, County Offaly, Ireland.*
Eleventh century AD.

Today there is a great revival of things Celtic. The arts, crafts, music, literature, folklore and history are all represented. This has primarily been fostered by people in the Celtic countries, but also by dedicated people worldwide who feel a common bond with the Celtic spirit.

13

Celtic crafts utilize many different media. There are workers in pottery, stained glass, precious metals, leather, stone, enamel, wood and much more. All are producing beautiful objects. The designs used are based mainly on patterns found in the great illuminated Gospels of Kells and Lindisfarne. However, more creative artists are producing new designs using the original Celtic methods of construction. A few contemporary artists and craftworkers have taken the La Tène designs of the early Celtic era and created new and exciting work based on these.

Celtic music is widely known and loved by many. Instruments such as the harp, various styles of pipes such as Uilleann (Irish) and Northumbrian, the Irish bodhrán or hand-drum, the fiddle and the Breton bombarde are among those used to fine effect. Nowadays all styles are represented, from early traditional to folk-rock.

Celtic languages are enjoying a welcome revival. Written and verbal Scots Gaelic, Irish, Welsh and Breton are all on the increase, and there is now a full Cornish dictionary available (the Cornish language was in danger of vanishing completely several decades ago).

In all, the spirit of the Celt is very much alive and well. Their ancient belief systems, based around the natural cycle of the year, are also being studied and utilized by many who find that the pace of Western life today has alienated them from contact with the natural world and the turning of the seasons. People are realizing that a return to Mother Earth in all Her glories has a healing and uplifting effect on the psyche, and a sense of wonder is gradually returning, to the benefit of all concerned.

Images such as the Green Man, the archetypal spirit of nature, or Cernunnos – Lord of the Animals, as he was known to the early Celts – are encouraging a greater respect for nature and all living things. The earliest portrayal of Cernunnos is in the decoration of the exquisite Gundestrup Cauldron, a solid silver Celtic vessel excavated in Denmark, dating from the first century BC. Subsequently he is found carved as a human head surrounded by or peering through foliage in various medieval churches throughout Britain and Europe. To this day a number of old country inns continue to use the name, or variations such as Robin Hood (Robin of the Wood), Jack-in-the Green or the Green Giant.

The Green Man is one example of an ancient archetype returning to our awareness at a much-needed time, to inspire the preservation of the natural kingdom of our planet.

Celtic spirituality, as embodied by the early Celtic Christian Church, is now being seen as a welcome source of inspiration to some of the arid and dry 'Churchianity' of this century. Prior to AD 664 and the Synod of Whitby, which was a forceful imposition by the Roman Church, the original Christianity practised by the Celtic Church was very different from that of today. Calendar dates of Easter and other festivals were changed by the Synod, creating a belief system out of tune with the rhythms of nature. Prior to this event, women were on an equal footing with men in religious matters and marriage in the priesthood was quite acceptable. It is documented that several Celtic saints had wives and children.

This balanced and nature-orientated spirituality is now starting to be incorporated by certain elements of today's Church. Interestingly, just as Iona in the sixth century AD was at the forefront of Celtic Christianity, so the present-day Iona community is one of the pioneers of its revival. 'Green spirituality' is seen by many as the most viable vehicle for carrying Christianity into the twenty-first century, as well as fostering an ecological approach to our planet.

To conclude, we wish you beauty on your journey through these Celtic images and hope that they will inspire you to discover more about the fascinating world of the Celts.

David James
Portesham, Dorset

'The Painted Warrior'.

The Celtic Warrior
An Ancient Tradition

To OBTAIN the optimum overview on the world of the early Celts, two main avenues are available to us. First, there are the accounts of the Celts by classical writers. These include the ancient Greeks Diodorus Siculus, Polybius and Strabo, and the Romans Livy, Julius Caesar and Tacitus (Tacitus had his account from the Roman general Agricola, who was his father-in-law as well as being governor of Britain). All of these writings chronicle direct experiences of encounters with the Celts.

Carvings from the entrance stone of Newgrange
chambered cairn, County Meath, Ireland, c. 3200 BC.

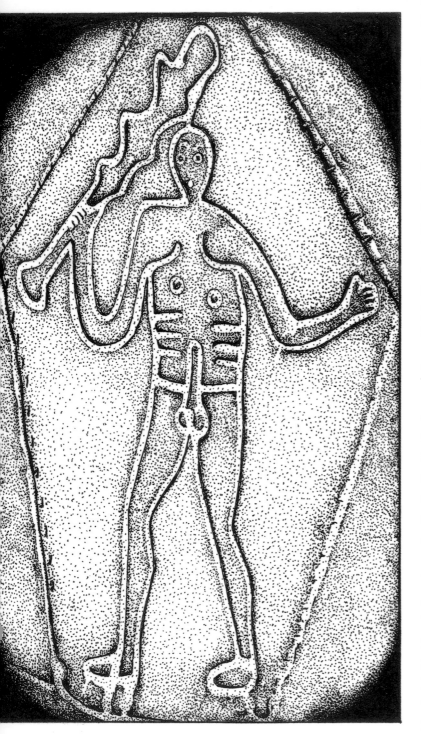

The Cerne giant. A warrior/fertility figure carved into chalk hillside above Cerne Abbas, Dorset. It is 180 ft (55 metres) in length.

The second avenue is archaeological evidence from this early time. Artefacts discovered over the centuries are now carefully preserved in museums worldwide. Excavations of burial chambers, mounds and even complete Celtic villages have provided invaluable information.

Both these sources tell us that from the earliest Celtic times, the Celts were superb horsemen and fierce warriors. Their horsemanship was said to be unsurpassed. Until about the fifth century BC, fighting was carried out on foot or on horseback, using wooden spears tipped with metal. During the fifth century the horse-drawn chariot, a formidable vehicle for warfare, was employed by the Celts. They subsequently terrorized every area they raided, including northern Italy, Greece and eventually France (Gaul). These Celtic tribes also occupied their own territories and fought among themselves. Each individual tribe had its own leader, who in turn possessed a personal adviser or seer on whom the tribe relied for much guidance.

Regarding Celtic horsemanship, in *The Gallic Wars* Julius Caesar says:

Such is the manoeuvrability of their chariots, as a result of thorough daily training they are capable of controlling their teams at full gallop down a steep, even precipitous slope, and stopping or turning them on a coin. They are also in the habit of running along the pole, standing on the yoke, and regaining the safety of their chariot again at top speed.

The earliest warrior image in Britain, pre-dating the chariot era considerably, is the Cerne giant. This is to be found at Cerne Abbas in Dorset and is a 180-foot-long (55-metre) figure cut into the chalk hillside. Some think he is possibly related to the pagan god Helis: others say he is a form of Cernunnos, Lord of the Animals. He is also very much an early symbol of fertility, with his large, erect phallus. Some archaeol-

*A bronze from Llyn Cerrig Bach, Anglesey, with Gallic coin,
from the first century BC, as inset.*

A free-standing Celtic slab cross at Fahan Mura, County Donegal, Ireland.

ogists date him as early as 1500 BC, though he is almost certainly not so old.

From the fifth century onwards, the horse is much represented in Celtic metalwork. We find La Tène bronze shields with images of horse and rider; early Celtic coins also carry designs of chariots, as well as of horses with and without armed riders. The chariot was also used in Britain, and there is a fine reconstruction in the National Museum of Wales in Cardiff of a Celtic chariot found in a peat bog at Llyn Cerrig Bach on Anglesey, dating from the first century AD. An earlier representation of the chariot appears on the Gundestrup Cauldron.

'Celtic Warrior'.

During the La Tène era swords and shields were made from iron and bronze, exhibiting elaborate and beautiful decoration. Helmets with pointed spikes were also favoured. All these marvellously crafted metal artefacts of warfare were primarily made for and used by high-ranking members of Celtic tribes. Plain wooden shields consisting of two joined pieces of wood were used by ordinary warriors. Of headgear, Diodorus Siculus writes: 'They have bronze helmets with tall crests, which give their wearers the appearance of enormous height.'

The horses themselves were provided with protective bronze masks, which in themselves are superb examples of Celtic metalwork, having 'horns' projecting from the front of them. Woe betide anyone finding themselves in the way! Horse harnesses had elaborately worked metal decorations, and a number of these have been discovered in Celtic chariot burials. Leading Celtic warriors were interred beside their own chariot, with their sword, shield and other weaponry. A number of these sites have been excavated in Britain and Europe, including a fine one at Garton Slack, Humberside. This contained dismantled chariot wheels with metal 'tyres', bridle bits and horse fittings.

Despite the warfaring nature of the Celts, great pride was taken in the artistic decoration of weaponry. Swords and sword sheaths were often engraved with fine spiral ornamentation; belt buckles and helmets too were often embellished with fine designs. Some of the most beautiful La Tène metalwork is in the form of bronze shields, which were embossed with bold curves and spiral motifs. Some also bore figures of horses and horsemen. One of the finest La Tène shields was dredged from the River Thames

An illuminated letter from the Saltair na Rann; eighth century AD. It is now in the Bodleian Library, Oxford.

in London and is known as the Battersea Shield. It is a later example, dating from early first century AD. The design consists of simple but powerful flowing curves, and the central bosses contain red enamel.

The Celtic custom of painting the body with a dye called woad, along with the use of metal trumpets to create a loud noise, must have made these people a ferocious spectacle in battle. Of the British Celts, Caesar writes in *The Gallic Wars*:

All Britons paint themselves with woad, which turns the skin a bluish-grey colour: hence their appearance is all the more horrific in battle. They grow their hair long, and shave every part of their body except the top of the head and the upper lip.

Well worth noting is the prowess of women in Celtic warfare. The classical writer Ammianus Marcellinus writes of the Celt and his wife: 'she was stronger than he was, and could rain blows and kicks upon the assailants equal in force to the shots of a catapult.' The notable British queen Boudicca, chief of the Iceni, the Celtic tribe occupying what is now Norfolk and Suffolk, was certainly a force to be reckoned with. As Dio Cassius wrote: 'She was huge of frame and terrifying of aspect, with a harsh voice. A great mass of red hair fell to her knees.' When seen driving her chariot,

Figures from the Gundestrup Cauldron, Denmark; first to second century BC.

Left: A warrior carving. One of a group of early Celtic carvings found on White Island, County Fermanagh, Ireland. Eighth century AD.

she must have presented a most awesome picture! From all this we can deduce that in general the Celts were a fearsome people, virtually unstoppable in battle. This was shown by their invasions of Rome in 390 BC and Delphi in 279 BC. Only the might of the Roman army was capable of subduing them, and by 50 BC the western Celtic world was under Roman dominion as far as the English Channel.

At this point we should ask how such wild and warfaring people managed to incorporate beautiful craftwork into their daily life.

The answer to this can be found by examining the personality of European Celts. Classical writers reveal that their overriding trait was flamboyance. They were, if you like, the Gary Glitters of the first millennium BC, and most certainly if Harley Davidsons had been in existence, they would have been riding them!

Starting with personal appearance, there was a particular fashion whereby men rinsed their hair in a wash of lime and pulled it into a spiky 'mane' so that when it dried they resembled a fierce animal. Another style was to part the hair in the centre and tie the top portion into a knot which sat on the crown of the head. Diodorus Siculus writes of the Celts that they

wear striking clothing, tunics dyed and embroidered in many colours, and trousers which they call 'bracae'; and they wear striped cloaks fastened by a brooch, thick in winter and light in summer, worked in a many-hued, closely set check pattern.

From this it can be seen that no ordinary sword, shield or chariot decoration would satisfy the extrovert nature of the Celts. Their idea of a horse's head protection

Opposite: A composite picture using the Gundestrup Cauldron as a basis. The horse wearing a bronze champfrein from the first century BC is in the centre.

was not just a functional piece of metal which the horse was able to see through; it had to be striking, even fearsome in appearance, and was designed to 'stand out from the crowd'. Small items such as cloak pins or belt buckles were not just practical; they needed to be well constructed and eye-catching. The process of enamelling was known to the Celts, the colour red being the most popular. Horses' harness mounts were sometimes made of bronze inlaid with red enamel, and a fine pair from the first century AD were found in Polden Hills in Somerset. Swords and sword scabbards exist with a wide variety of elaborate ornamentation, from finely detailed cross-hatching to swirling curves and spirals. No doubt the whole regalia was part of the psychology of Celtic warfare. Imagine the feelings of terror evoked when the Celts suddenly descended in this fashion on a quiet village settlement. No doubt the first reaction of the inhabitants would have been 'flight' rather than 'fight'.

The construction of these metal artefacts would not have proved a problem to knowledgeable craftsmen. The materials and equipment to make them would have been light enough to adapt to a travelling lifestyle. A small chariot could easily carry a few bags of scrap bronze, iron ingots and even crushed glass, which when heated and melted could produce an effect similar to enamel.

A further personality trait was that the Celts had no fear of death. A belief in rebirth was firmly established, and was the main reason why they fought with such ferocity. They believed implicitly that, should they be killed, their souls would be reborn automatically. Imagining life at that time, and the importance even to a warfaring people of the cycle of the seasons, this belief is not hard to understand. Every year the trees shed their leaves, the flowers withered and once winter had set in there was little sign of life from Mother Earth. Yet with the coming of spring, rebirth occurred, new green shoots and buds appeared; trees and plants which were seemingly dead miraculously came to life again. If this happened in nature, then surely it must happen in human beings as well.

The Cult of the Head, which to us today seems rather gruesome, was practised by some warfaring Celts. The soul of a person was said to reside in the head. Thus when captives were slain, they were beheaded and their heads brought back to the encampment. Behind this was the

An elaborately engraved bronze scabbard from Lisnacrogher, County Antrim, Northern Ireland.

belief that the soul and the intelligence of the captive would then
assist the captors in their further exploits. Grim but true!

The human head was also believed to possess oracular and
prophetic powers. As a result, this cult was elaborated on in certain
parts of Europe, where shrines were constructed housing the heads
of rulers or wise people. Alcoves were cut in a stone dolmen and the
heads placed within. These were then venerated, in the belief that
the dead person's knowledge would be imparted to the suppli-
cant. One such shrine containing several human heads existed
at Roquepertuse, in Bouches de Rhône, France.

This chapter has given some insight into the nature and
psychology of the Celtic peoples from the Hallstatt era of
around 700 BC up to the time of the Roman invasion of
Britain in AD 43. Not long after this event, the many
Celtic tribes in Britain, from the Catuvellauni, who
lived surrounding what is now the London area, to the
Brigantes, who lived north of the Humber estuary,
were scattered. Only Ireland, remote parts of Scotland,
especially the west coast and its islands, as well as
remote and wild areas of Wales, Cornwall and Brittany
remained as Celtic strongholds.

A handgrip extension from a shield found with the Sutton Hoo ship burial.
Seventh century AD.

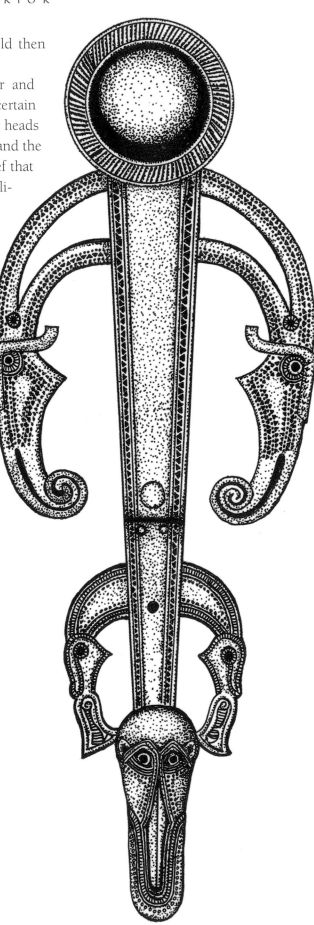

'King of the Fishes'.

The Kingdom of Nature
Celts and the Living World

TO GAIN some understanding of the relationship that the Celts had with nature, we should try to take ourselves back in time to the first millennium BC.

If you close your eyes and endeavour to imagine what life in general would have been like at that time, an interesting picture will emerge. There are no mechanized forms of transport, so there are no roads as we know them. There is no electricity, so the vast array of equipment associated with this energy form is non-existent — no TV, radio, telephone, lighting or any of the other associated benefits we have today.

As to living itself, there are no building contractors and there is no machinery, so whatever you need has to be constructed by you, alone or with the help of friends, out of locally occurring natural materials. Where you build is also important, as there is obviously no running water laid on. Being near a spring or stream is a necessity.

Light is another important factor. When it starts to get dark, you can't just reach out for the nearest light switch, so the main feature of the day is the sun. When it rises and when it sets dictate your pattern of activity. Likewise the sun (or lack of it) dictates the seasons, and your daily period of activity will be much longer in summer than in winter, when it gets dark earlier. Clocks and watches are obviously non-existent, so the sun (or the intensity of daylight) will give you an idea of the time of day. This vast yellow orb in the sky seems to rule your existence to a very large extent.

Imagine, for example, living on a hillside and looking out over a distant view. No roads, no concrete or brick buildings, no pylons, no aeroplanes in the sky. Just you and the natural world. Thus in peaceful times your most immediate relationships are with things that to us in the twentieth century might at first seem a little bizarre but to you in that era are very important.

Mother Earth gives you food and likewise permits you to drink Her water. (No superstores or soft-drinks machines.) Magical and wonderful living entities called trees grow in Her soil. They provide shelter, building materials, firewood and natural remedies for illnesses, and above all you know that they live a longer time than yourself, so they are much revered. Evergreen trees, especially the yew, which has the potential to live indefinitely, were the most highly revered and it was forbidden to cut off any of their branches. Several of today's yews are some 4,000 years old, according to yew-tree expert Allen Meredith. The sacred nature of the yew tree is an entire topic in itself, but as an idea of their sanctity, a number of early churches in Britain were built close to already ancient yew trees. Until recently, this was thought to be the other way round, but research by Allen Meredith, assisted by David Bellamy and others, has proved conclusively that the trees preceded the churches.[1]

Detail from the Gundestrup Cauldron; first to second century BC.

No traffic of any kind and minimal numbers of people except for your own tribe, so when you are out and about (which is most of the time, as you need to hunt for food, gather firewood and have a host of other daily tasks to perform) you notice what is around you – and that is the animal kingdom. In all of what are known today as the Celtic countries, there are salmon rivers. At a certain time of year the salmon come upstream to spawn. This is a most spectacular sight and must explain why the salmon was felt to be worthy of much veneration, as well as being a sacred source of food.

Deer roamed the countryside in profusion, mainly because in those days there was much more woodland to give them shelter. Wild boar also existed in these woods. They must have provided quite an awesome sight, with their tusks and pointed snouts. In the sky the eagle was the dominant bird. Most Celtic countries being mountainous, they were well populated with the golden eagle, the mountain forests being their nesting grounds. Watching an eagle hovering at great height before swooping down on its prey may seem just a 'nice' image to us today, surrounded as we are by so many twentieth-century distractions, but to the early Celts this would have been a very powerful experience and would have remained in the mind for quite some time afterwards.

We must not forget the horse, the animal closest to the Celtic peoples. Used for both pulling chariots in war and long-distance travel in peacetime, the horse was the Celts' most prized and revered possession. Having built up a very special relationship with their horses, the Celts, as we have already seen, were considered the ultimate horsemen. Not surprisingly, then, we find that there was a Celtic

A woodcarving from Felbach-Smidden, Germany; first to second century BC.

horse cult. This featured the horse goddess Epona, symbolized by a white mare. Carvings and votive offerings in the form of bronze, clay and wooden horses have been found associated with Celtic sites in Europe as early as the eighth century BC. This cult led, at a considerably later date, to the carvings of white horses into the landscape. A notable British example is at Uffington in Oxfordshire, where the present carving, said by some archaeologists to date from the ninth century AD, is believed to be superimposed on one of a much earlier date.

The horse goddess Epona, a Gallo-Roman carving, and the White Horse of Uffington, near Oxford.

So, we can build up a reasonable picture of the life of the early Celts in relation to their surroundings, and from the above it is not surprising that trees and animals, earth and water, and the sun all featured so very powerfully in their belief system. Each had a spirit of its own and required special respect and veneration. From this it is quite understandable that there should be a supreme figure presiding over the nature kingdom. In the first millennium BC he was known as Cernunnos, Lord of the Animals. An image on the Gundestrup Cauldron shows him with antlers on his head, sitting cross-legged and holding a torc in his right hand and a serpent in his left. Representations of Cernunnos occur in other parts of Europe and in some regions he was known as the stag god. He was considered the ruler of the natural kingdom in all its aspects of life, death and rebirth. This archetype reappears at a later date in many cultures, different names expressing very similar beliefs. For example, the Green Man, Pan, Jack-in-the-Green and

'The Far-sighted One'.

Robin Hood are images found mainly in Britain; in Germany he was known as the Wild Man; the Gypsies knew him as Green George; and in Sweden he was known a the Pfingstl. These essences are still incorporated in the folk-beliefs of today, and medieval carvings of the Green Man can be found in various churches and cathedrals throughout Britain and Europe.

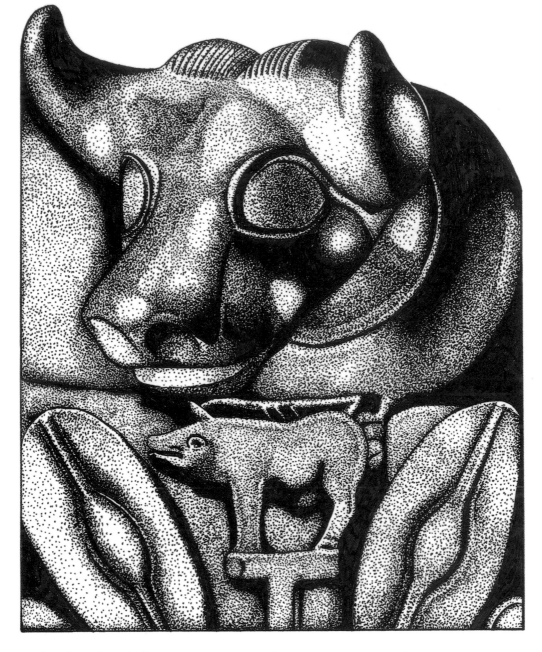

A boar from 'The Arch of Narbonne' and the image of a bull on a cauldron mount from Jutland, Denmark.

It is interesting to consider the phrase 'Mother Earth'. In doing so, we find that long before the Christian era, 'deity' as such was always female. This can be traced back to some of the earliest sculptures in existence. The abundance and fertility of Mother Earth naturally lends itself to a goddess-centred belief system, and the earth itself was considered a womb in which seeds, when planted, would eventually grow to living plants and trees. The Cornish 'fogous' were man-made underground chambers to facilitate communion with the Earth Mother, using appropriate ritual. Goddess figures are

'Entwined Dogs'.

known as far back as the palaeolithic era, and several carvings, including the famous one from Willendorf in Austria, have been dated to *c.* 30,000 BC. During the first millennium BC the Celtic belief system evolved, incorporating both god and goddess figures, and even in the Christian era some saints, such as St Bride, have their origins firmly rooted in pagan Celtic goddess figures.

Returning to Cernunnos, we find sadly that the Lord of the Animals was much misrepresented by the early Roman Church, and in the fourth century BC St Augustine wrote of 'a most filthy habit of dressing up as a horse or a stag'. The constructed image of the Christian devil with his horns is almost certainly a distortion of pre-existing nature deities such as Cernunnos and Pan. Nevertheless, Cernunnos survives in the form of the Green Man, embodied in folklore, folk-dances, legends and carvings throughout the Western world. Place-names too give an indication of his existence: for example, 'Cerne' of Cerne Abbas in Dorset (the 'Abbas' was a later addition in early medieval monastic times).

As for animals themselves, they were held in great esteem by the early Celts. It was not so much the animal but its essential energy or spirit that featured in their belief system. With the Celtic belief in 'shape-shifting', the gods were said to be able to appear in animal form as they chose.

The boar was ferocious and fearsome to look at. When cornered, it would fight to the last and so its essence was venerated in battle; it was believed to make warriors more ferocious. Several bronze helmets have been found

The symbols of the Evangelists from the Book of Armagh, an eighth-century Irish illuminated Gospel.

with boars modelled at the topmost point. Boars are also found on bronze shields, and there are some fine free-standing sculptures, including one made from bronze discovered at Neuvy-en-Sullias in France, dating from the first century BC.

The salmon, king of the fishes, was also held in great esteem. The fish that had the knowledge to come upstream each year against the current to spawn in the shallows, and whose scales shone with a lustrous pearl hue, was seen as the embodiment of wisdom. This iconography continued into the Celtic Christian era, when the fish was used as the symbol of Christ.

The Picts, the indigenous inhabitants of the eastern regions of Scotland, used these animals in their stone-carvings. There is a fine salmon on the reverse side of the Glamis Cross, which dates from the early eighth century AD. Likewise a fragment of a Pictish carving from the same era, found at Dores, Inverness-shire, portrays a wild boar.

The bull, symbol of masculinity and fertility, as well as of strength, is found in early Gaulish carvings and was subsequently adopted by the Romans in their worship of Mithras.

The stag occurs as sculpture and ornament throughout Europe associated with the early Celts. For them this animal symbolized the essence of the spirit of nature at peace in the wild[2] and was also associated with Cernunnos. The deer too occurs in late Pictish carvings of the fifth to eighth centuries AD in north-east Scotland.

The eagle (or hawk) was seen as a symbol of vision and far-sightedness and as such was a bird treated with great respect. The eagle's spirit was also said to possess prophetic powers. It is interesting to note that the fish, the eagle and the bull are all carried through into Christian symbolism. In the great illuminated Gospels the eagle is portrayed as the symbol of St John and the bull, now become a calf, as the symbol of St Luke.

In Irish mythology birds were often represented as having supernatural powers. The swan (as in the saga *The Children of Lir*), the raven, the owl and other birds all have special attributes and a distinctive mythology surrounding them.

Fortunately one aspect of today's revival of 'green spirituality', based on the Celtic Christian beliefs before the influence of the Roman Church, takes into strong account the divine aspect of the kingdom of nature. Even though such figures as Cernunnos, Pan and the Green Man are not directly represented, their essence is most certainly there, embodied in the respect for all living things. This essence is by no means limited to Celtic Christianity; parallels may be drawn with various cultures and belief systems, including Buddhism and American Indian spirituality.

Centuries of Craftsmanship
Celtic Metalwork

CELTIC METALWORK, from the La Tène era and even earlier, through to the late Celtic Christian period, is a subject close to the hearts of many people. Some of the finest craftsmanship in the world was produced by the Celts, and to cover the whole topic many books would be required. Here we will touch on the best-known examples, as well as some of the more unusual styles and artefacts. These artefacts are on display in museums world-wide, providing a wealth of fine examples of Celtic craftsmanship.

Mention Celtic jewellery at the time of the Roman conquest of Britain and one particular item springs to many people's minds. This is the torc. The torc was a circular band, often made from several separate strands of metal twisted together. Torcs did not join up to form a complete circle. Instead, the two ends or finials were usually elaborately decorated. The fact that they did not join also made them adjustable, so that they could be fitted around the arm, leg or neck of the wearer.

Torcs were very much a symbol of wealth and status. A Celtic chief would have had a torc made from gold or silver, whereas for lower orders they would have been made from bronze. The torc was also said to be a symbol of divinity, and, as we have seen, the image of Cernunnos on the Gundestrup Cauldron shows him holding a torc in his right hand. The Roman historian Dio Cassius describes Boudicca, queen of the Iceni Celts, as riding into battle 'wearing a great twisted golden necklace'.

Torcs of fine quality were made throughout Europe in the latter part of the first millennium BC. It is thought that in Britain their manufacture was almost entirely restricted to the region of East Anglia, then the territory of the Iceni. Discoveries at Snettisham in Norfolk have provided torcs of superb craftsmanship and also of immense value. Between 1948 and 1950, in a series of excavations, fifty-eight torcs were found in this region. The largest is made from electrum and is about 8 inches (20 cm) in diameter. A number of smaller ones of gold and silver have been discovered in the same region. Torcs might have been made in other parts of Britain but in very

Opposite: The cumdach *of Molaise's Gospels from Ireland dates from the eighth century* AD.

A Celtic bronze torc, second century BC.

limited quantities, and some which have been discovered in hoards containing other precious artefacts and coins are thought to have originated from overseas.

In the chapter on Celtic warriors we mentioned the La Tène bronze shields, swords, helmets, horses' head masks or *champfreins* and accompanying bridle and chariot bronze decorations, all of which were executed with great skill and sometimes decorated with enamel work.

Another favourite of the flamboyant Celts was the bronze mirror, numerous examples of which have been found in Britain and Europe. They were made until the first century AD, and consisted of a circular disc of bronze with a decorated metal handle. One side would have been highly polished and without decoration. The reverse side gave the craftsman adequate opportunity to display his design skills. Bold curves and spirals are most frequently used, typical of the La Tène style, with very finely detailed cross-hatching to fill in some of the larger areas. Old Warden in Bedfordshire, Desborough in Northamptonshire and Birdlip in Gloucestershire are three places which have yielded exceptionally impressive mirrors.

The Hunterston Brooch; silver, gold and amber. This dates from the seventh century AD, *with tenth-century Scandinavian runes carved on the reverse.*

A detail of a bronze Celtic mirror from Holcombe, Devon.

Fine examples of bronze Celtic sculptures have been discovered in Europe, with representations of horse and chariots, wild boar, horses and other animals, including dogs. At Neuvy-en-Sullias in France, on the banks of the River Loire, a hoard of small, beautifully cast bronze figurines was discovered opposite the Celtic shrine of Fleury. These show men and women dancing, and may portray a sacred ritual. A bronze head from Bouvray in France shows a Celtic deity. This piece is most elegant, and the male head is shown with a torc around his neck.

In some cases metalwork was combined with wood: for example, in the making of tankards and drinking vessels. Interestingly, one of the best surviving British examples comes from Trawsfynydd in Wales and is lined with yew. Bearing in mind the sacred nature of the yew, the vessel was probably fashioned for ceremonial rather than domestic use.

Larger vessels for holding liquids, mostly constructed from silver, were another favourite of the Celts. The Gundestrup Cauldron has already been mentioned and is probably the finest decorated silver Celtic vessel of that era. Another rather smaller silver example, said to have been made in Europe and dating from the same time, was discovered early this century in a chieftain's grave at Welwyn in Hertfordshire. Cauldrons appear in many Celtic legends, and to drink from them or to be immersed in them was said to produce an altered state of awareness. Analogies have been made with the Christian font and baptism.[3]

Returning to the Gundestrup Cauldron briefly, part of the fine decoration contains an image of Taranis, the Celtic god of the wheel. We have already discussed the use of the chariot by the Celts. It is also believed that the

A cast bronze arm ring from Czechoslovakia; second century BC.

4 3

spoked (rather than the solid) wheel was a Celtic invention. This certainly streamlined and improved its efficiency. Taranis was known as 'the thunderer', presumably from the noise of a chariot heading into battle. The name has its roots in the Welsh word '*taran*', meaning thunder.

After the Roman invasion of Britain in AD 43 there was a mixing of cultures and styles, and soon what would previously have been described as Celtic became an inferior art form known as Romano-Celtic. To find our way back to true Celtic metalwork, it is necessary to look at the beginnings of the Celtic monastic system in Ireland, and in those areas such as western Scotland and west Wales where the searfaring Irish monks and their descendants established monastic communities.

The era of sacred Irish metal work is held by some to be the most creative time in the history of world art. Beginning in the late fourth century AD and continuing until the tenth century, it has certainly produced some of the finest individual pieces of work the world has ever known. This period also covers the creation of the great illuminated Gospels. The Books of Durrow and Armagh were produced in Ireland, the Book of Kells was produced by Irish monks on Iona, and the Book of Lindisfarne was also created by Irish

Taranis, god of the wheel, from the Gundestrup Cauldron and a chariot figure from Scania, Sweden, dating from the first to the second century BC.

Detail from the Gundestrup Cauldron and the Rynkeby Cauldron, Denmark; second century BC.

monks on Holy Island, off the coast of Northumbria. Also at this time the Celtic high crosses of Ireland, western Scotland and Wales were carved.

The craftsmen of this era were highly skilled. They were fully conversant not only with the techniques of working with precious metals and enamels but also with the geometric and mathematical construction of complex designs. This geometric basis has been re-created for us this century by the painstaking and lifelong efforts of the Scottish artist, illustrator and writer George Bain, whose work forms the basis for the art and craftwork of many Celtic artists today.[4]

The knotwork, spirals and key patterns found as decoration on sacred Irish metalwork follow a strict geometric formula and it was only when this had been fully completed that the craftsmen could continue the ornamentation 'freehand'.

It is not known where this geometric-based art form originated. It was certainly also used by the Picts of northern and eastern Scotland, and has some parallels with Islamic and Near Eastern art. There is a possibility that in

Detail from the Ardagh chalice. Silver, decorated with gold and bronze ornamentation with glass and enamel studs.

simplified form it may have arrived in Ireland via the Phoenician Trading Route at a very early date, and was subsequently elaborated on by the Irish monks.

By the sixth century AD the art form was well established, and beautiful artefacts were being made in bronze and precious metals by highly skilled craftsmen.

The words of Giraldus Cambrensis (Gerald of Wales) might be appropriate here. He was a travelling ecclesiastic in the late twelfth and early thirteenth centuries. In 1181 he journeyed around Wales, keeping a diary as he went. It seems that he was inspired by the experience, as a few years later he made

The cumdach *of Molaise's Gospels from Devenish Island, County Fermanagh, Ireland; eighth century* AD.

An engraved disc from Donore, County Meath, Ireland; seventh century AD.

a similar journey through Ireland which he also documented. While in Kildare he was shown a copy of one of the illuminated Gospels and his comments, written in Latin at the time, could just as easily have been applied to much of the Celtic metalwork of that period:

If you take the trouble to look very closely, and penetrate with your eyes the secrets of the artistry, you will notice such intricacies, so delicate and subtle, so close together and well knitted, so involved and bound together . . . that you will not hesitate to declare that all these things must have been the work, not of men, but of angels.[5]

Certainly, if one examines carefully such treasures as the Derrynaflan chalice, dating to the early ninth century AD, this description seems quite appropriate.

The setting for this burst of supreme creativity should be considered, and compared with the tribal structure of the European and early British Celts of

A crucifixion plaque from Rinnagan, County Roscommon, Ireland. Copper alloy, eighth century AD.

pre-Roman times. The Irish monastic system in the main encompassed a very peaceful if austere lifestyle. Much time was given to contemplation; also the arts and crafts were held in high esteem. Compared with the warfaring nature of their earlier counterparts, the Irish Celtic monks had created an ideal environment for their detailed and very sophisticated craftwork. As every artefact of an ecclesiastical nature was made 'for the greater glory of God', no time limits were imposed. This contrasts with the early Celts, whose bold and flamboyant craftwork was mainly required for times of warfare.

There are books available solely on the subject of Irish Celtic metalwork,[6] so it will suffice here to describe just a few of the most spectacular items. Being fashioned in a religious context, these are mostly connected with church ritual.

Two superb chalices exist, both dating from the early ninth century AD, the Ardagh and the Derrynaflan chalices. Both are fashioned from silver, with exquisite gold filigree Celtic ornamentation around the base, stem and bowl. The gold is inset with polished amber. The Derrynaflan chalice was discovered in 1980 within a monastic site in County Tipperary, along with a gold-embellished silver paten and foot-ring, and a silver ladle-strainer with cloisonné enamel decoration. The Ardagh chalice may well have been

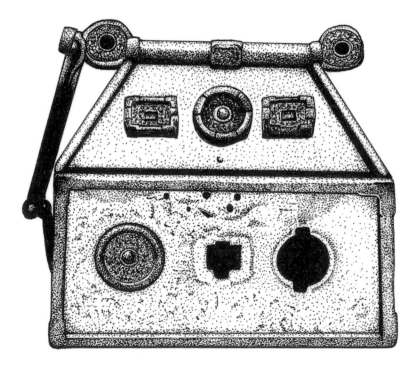

The Monymusk reliquary. This is believed to have contained relics of St Columba. Silver, copper alloy and yew. Scottish, eighth century AD.

made by the same craftsmen: its profuse, finely detailed gold ornamentation has to be seen to be believed. Even the base of the foot is
engraved with wonderful spirals of an elaborate and highly complex
design.

Another religious artefact which should be mentioned is the reliquary. This was a small, portable house-shaped shrine containing
a relic of a saint or holy person. They were made from copper,
silver or bronze, with prolific Celtic decoration inlaid with enamels
and semiprecious stones such as garnet, amber and carnelian.
Again the sacred nature of the yew tree appears, as almost all
known examples have a wooden interior fashioned from a single
block of yew. Examples from Lough Erne, County Fermanagh,
and Monymusk in Scotland date from the eighth century AD.

The crozier or bishop's staff was another religious object
which received elaborate and exquisite metalwork decoration. The curved end or crook was often encased in metal
with very elaborate and beautiful Celtic designs.
A number of Irish examples exist, mostly from the eighth
century AD.

The processional cross, made from bronze or silver and
wonderfully ornamented, was another artefact of exquisite
beauty created by Irish craftsmen. This was usually
mounted on a wooden pole, the cross itself being about
2 feet (60 cm) in height. The finest example is the
ninth-century-AD Cross of Cong. Both of its sides
are profusely decorated with very detailed Celtic
ornamentation.

Extremely fine Celtic ornamentation can also be
found on bell-shrines. These are bronze, four-sided

St Patrick's bell-shrine. Now in the Museum of the Royal Irish Academy, Dublin; c. AD 1100.

cases of similar shape to the bell that they contain. They were preserved as holy relics containing an artefact which belonged to a particular saint. The shrine of the Bell of St Patrick's
Will is probably the finest example of several which still exist, and dates from between 1091
and 1105. It has wonderfully elaborate designs on the four sides and 'crown', and is decorated with gold, silver, enamel and semiprecious stones. It is now in the museum of the
Royal Irish Academy in Dublin. The early Celtic bell was looked upon with the highest
veneration and was used in ceremonies for healing the sick, as an aid to victory in battle and
in the solemnizing of sacred vows. These practices almost certainly have their roots in
pre-Christian Celtic culture.

Crucifixion plaques were also made in the eighth and ninth centuries AD in Ireland. These
were elaborately decorated with spirals and Celtic ornamentation, and cast from a copper

alloy. The faces on these plaques bear a strong resemblance to sculptures of the pre-Christian era. One of the finest was discovered on an ecclesiastical site at Rinnagan, County Westmeath. Approximately 9 inches (23 cm) high, it dates from the eighth century AD. A remarkably similar carving of a crucifixion scene of similar age and style but engraved in stone was discovered in a ruined Celtic chapel on the Isle of Man and is known as the Calf of Man Crucifixion stone.[7]

In Scotland also, magnificent metal artefacts have been discovered in ecclesiastical sites. Some of the best known are contained in the St Ninian's Isle hoard, uncovered in 1958 in the Shetland Isles. All the artefacts were discovered beneath a stone slab within the ruins of an early church. It is very likely that they were hidden here during a Viking raid on the island – Viking raids from the seventh to the tenth centuries AD were frequent and also extremely brutal. This was the one thing that the Celtic monks of both Ireland and Scotland would have feared. Many Irish and outlying Scottish monastic sites were raided at this period, including Iona, which was invaded several times. The monks often managed to conceal their ecclesiastical treasures, though they themselves were frequently less fortunate!

The St Ninian's Isle hoard dates from around AD 800 and the style of design is Pictish, having strong links with Celtic art forms. There is a fine silver alloy bowl with a gold filigree centre inlaid with amber. It is interesting to note that among the hoard a box was discovered made of larch, containing the jawbone of a porpoise. Larch being a sacred evergreen tree, this was obviously a very special item. Nowadays much research is being carried out with regard to the healing powers, as well as the advanced states of consciousness, of dolphins and porpoises. It seems possible that our Celtic ancestors were already aware of these special qualities.

One further item of Irish jewellery that must be

The Cross of Cong. Decoration from an elaborate portable bronze cross made for the King of Connach, c. AD 1123, and said to enshrine a relic of the original Cross.

Crook of the Kells Crozier, which is now in the British Museum. Bronze, tenth to eleventh century AD.

mentioned is the penannular brooch. Certain examples are classed as among the finest jewellery ever made. At this time the main item of clothing was the cloak, made from heavy and substantial material. To secure this, a fastening was required which was robust and long-lasting, as well as being visually attractive. Seventh–ninth-century-AD Irish metalworkers excelled at these brooches, and fortunately there are a considerable number still in existence, on display in museums today. Probably the most famous of them all is the Tara brooch, found at Bettystown, County Meath, and dating from the eighth century AD. This piece of jewellery certainly fits Gerald of Wales's description as being 'the work of angels' with its fantastically intricate Celtic design in sunken gold filigree, cloisonné enamel bosses and interlacing bird motifs. Penannular brooches were made with a strong pin 4–6 inches (10–15 cm) long to ensure secure fastening of the cloak. These brooches were made for both sacred and secular high-ranking people who could afford them. Penannular brooches were also made in Scotland with Pictish ornamentation. These were of the same shape and very similar in most details to the Irish brooches, and as some seem to be 'hybrids', incorporating both styles, it is possible that there was contact between the two schools of craftsmen. Some of the finest Pictish penannular brooches were found in the St Ninian's Isle hoard in the Shetland Isles, mentioned earlier.

One fine penannular brooch was found at Hunterston in Ayrshire, Scotland. It dates from the late seventh century AD, and has interesting tenth-century-AD Scandinavian runes engraved on the back. Other fine Irish examples are from Killamery, Roscrea and Ardagh. A number of brooches are embellished with polished amber, garnet, coloured glass and enamel.

For those fascinated by Celtic metalwork and jewellery, the era of Irish creativity from the sixth to the ninth centuries AD is well worth further investigation. The period has been rightly described by some as 'the golden age of creativity'.

We should not leave the subject of Celtic metalwork without some words on coinage. It is not known exactly when the Celts started to use coins as currency. Probably its introduction into the Celtic world was influenced by observations that both the Greek and the Roman civilizations used coins for trade. Previously, during the Hallstatt era, salt was the material used by the Celts as currency, as it was a scarce and very valuable commodity.

Later, as the Celts became a force to be reckoned with in battle, kings or city states were prepared to employ them as mercenaries and their payment was in the currency of that country.

Celtic coins have been discovered from most parts of Europe in small quantities. In Briain there were three main types in use prior to the Roman conquest. The gold stater was the most valuable. The decoration often incorporated a horse, with or without an armed rider, and sometimes a chariot. The majority of these gold coins date from between 50 and 25 BC and the design on some is remarkably abstract. The reason for this is not known, as the Celts were skilled craftsmen. Possibly there was some symbolic reason for the strange, almost 'cubist' designs.

For day-to-day transactions there was a lower-denomination silver coin. Again the designs on many of these are almost abstract. Perhaps they are stylizations to which we have lost the key. In one account by a Roman historian, we are told of warriors being paid one gold stater each for an entire campaign, which gives us some idea of their value!

Celtic coinage from Yugoslavia, first century BC.

Potin money was Celtic currency of an even smaller denomination. These coins were made from strips of tin alloy cut into individual units.

Cunobelinus was a great Celtic chieftain based at Camulodunum (later Colchester) between about AD 10 and AD 40. His coins bear a strong resemblance to Roman coins of the same era; it is not clear as to whether he designed his coinage to impress the Romans, with whom he must have had some contact, or was so impressed by their coinage that he decided to revise the style of his own. Some of the coins of Cunobelinus had the letters TASCO printed on them. This was an abbreviation of the name of his predecessor, Tascovianus, and the lettering was used to show that Cunobelinus was ruler. Like the Romans and also the Greeks, the Celts soon realized that coins, because they travelled far and wide, were an ideal medium for political propaganda.[8]

Celtic coins have a fascination all of their own, and fine examples can be seen today in museums throughout Britain and Europe.

Sacred Places
From Trees to Shrines

ONE OF THE KEY words that stands out in connection with the Celtic way of life is 'respect'. This incorporates a genuine expression of wonder and awe, so where better for Celts to experience these feelings than in the natural world surrounding them?

As has been said already, the earth was considered the Mother, the Giver and the Provider of Life; all Her aspects were revered.

Trees were a major source of inspiration and wonder. In the Seanchus Mor, the ancient Laws of Ireland, trees were divided into specific categories. There were the 'Chieftain trees', consisting of yew, oak, apple, ash, fir, hazel and holly. Then the 'Peasant trees', consisting of alder, birch, willow, aspen, hawthorn and elm. The third category was 'Shrub trees', consisting of black-thorn, spindle tree, elder, test tree, honeysuckle, bird cherry and white hazel. The fourth category was 'Herb trees', consisting of gorse, heather, broom, bog myrtle and rushes.

The system regarding these particular trees could well be implemented today with great effect, as each had a different 'honour price', payable as reparation if the tree received unauthorized injury or death. For major trees such as the yew and the oak, often used as tribal trees, capital punishment could be imposed; a fine of livestock was levied for desecrating minor trees.[9]

The yew tree was held especially sacred, and recent evidence[10] that it is the oldest living tree species in the world may well have already been known to the Celts. Ogham script, the early language of the Irish Celts, which is found carved on standing stones from the third century AD onwards, was said in Irish mythology to have been carved on pieces of yew wood long before this date. Both the tree and the individual ogham letter were said to possess magical properties; this is also reflected in the Norse culture, with their use of runes, which possessed both linguistic and magical characteristcs. A link with the yew tree and its divinatory powers of ogham

Opposite: 'The Sleeping Maiden'.

'Winter Solstice'.

can be made with an early medieval folk-custom in Britain. Young maidens would place a sprig of yew beneath their pillow on special days of the year. To observe this custom was said to induce a dream of their future sweetheart. At a later date we find yew wood used in the carving of sacred objects in the Celtic Christian Church, such as the reliquary, and the presence of the yew tree in early churchyards is a testament to its sacred nature. However, in the light of recent methodical research, it seems that the trees were often there long before the church itself.[11]

The oak is the other major tree associated with the Celts and their teachers, the druids. The Roman historian Pliny the Elder writes:

nothing is more sacred to the druids than the mistletoe and the tree on which it grows, especially if it be an oak. They choose oak woods for their sacred groves, and perform no sacred rite without using oak branches. Whatever grows on the tree is sent from heaven, a sign that the tree has been chosen by the god.

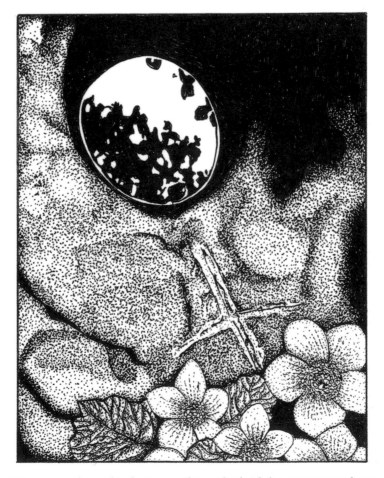

Bullaun stone, from Adrigole, County Clare, Ireland. A holy water-stoup with cross, carved into a natural boulder.

Shrine of St Non, above St Non's Well, Dyfed, Wales. St Non was the mother of St David, and the well has been used as a place of pilgrimage since the sixth century AD.

Vestiges of this cult are still to be found in Ireland, where coins are hammered into an ancient oak as offerings when requesting healing. Not so nice for the poor tree!

With the advent of Christianity to Ireland, the sacredness of the oak was preserved in place-names such as Kildare (*cille daire*), meaning 'church of the oaks'. The monastic site at Durrow comes from *daire maugh*, meaning 'plain of the oaks'. There are many more examples. To some of the more

St Abban's Grave, County Cork, Ireland.

'Waters of Life'.

dogmatic Christians, the significance of the oak grove was not understood and it was therefore considered to be outside their belief system. Consequently many were blessed and dedicated to the Virgin Mary, who was given the title Our Lady of the Oaks in early times.

Water has been held sacred since time immemorial, and the Celts certainly considered water to be the holy fluid of Mother Earth. Streams, rivers and especially springs and wells were revered. A number of surviving holy wells have a very old tree growing close by or right over them, combining the veneration of both wood and water.

Many of these wells had been sacred in their own right for several thousand years. With the advent of Christianity, they became associated with particular saints. Holy wells exist in all of the Celtic countries and many are still in use today. Often small stone shrines were built around them by the Celtic monks. An example of this is the sixth-century-AD well dedicated to St Seiriol at Penmon, on Anglesey. Some have later shrines surrounding them, constructed during the Middle Ages. Ireland, Wales, Cornwall,[12] Brittany and Scotland all have interesting examples, and there are also many to be found in Europe. Votive offerings have been discovered at the bottom of several holy wells which have been excavated. These range from very early goddess effigies to white quartz pebbles, coins and bronze ornaments. A notable example is the Well of the Triple Goddess at Minster, on the Isle of

Sheppey, where during recent excavations an early goddess figurine was found at the very bottom.[13]

One tradition, particularly strong in Ireland and Cornwall, that surrounds holy wells and survives to this day concerns the hanging of thin coloured strips of cloth in trees or bushes close to the well. It is based on the belief that a strip of cloth (known as a cloutie) from a sick person's garment, when hung close to the holy well, will soon disappear into the elements; the same, it is believed, would then happen with the illness of the afflicted person.

Hills, unusual shapes in the landscape and mountains all possessed their own guardians. Many mountains in the Celtic countries are named after gods or goddesses from the early Celtic sagas. For example, the beautiful mountainous area of the Cuillins on the Isle of Skye is named after the great champion of the Ulster heroes Cú Chulainn, and the mountains have many legends associated with him. Tumuli or ancient Bronze Age burial mounds

The Cuillin Mountains, Isle of Skye, western Scotland.

were seen as the home of the *sidhe* or 'the little people', who are much discussed in Evans Wentz's classic book *The Fairy Faith in Celtic Countries*.[14] Numerous stories and legends exist concerning the *sidhe* and their interactions with humans. Until recently there were quite frequently tales of people who passed by these tumuli at a certain time of the year or fell asleep beside them. They then describe how they were transported into the world of the *sidhe*, where they remained for many years, but on returning found that no time had elapsed at all. Folk-tales exist where the person emerges from the tumulus and his adventures with the *sidhe* to find that all his relatives are long since deceased, yet he has not aged at all. This kind of 'stepping out of time' may at first seem incredible, but it is interesting to note that it has occurred on a smaller scale quite recently during several documented 'encounters' with UFOs. This includes a television description given by a high-ranking American army official when investigating a UFO sighting in East Anglia. Checking his watch carefully and logging the time before he went to investigate the phenomenon, he found that after what appeared to be several hours of exploration on foot through dense woodland, when he finally returned to his vehicle, the time on his watch (US Army official issue) had not changed, although it was still working. Imagination, or a genuine 'shift out of time' like the encounters with the *sidhe*?

Opposite: *'Crowning of the Bard'*.

Standing stones at Callanish, Isle of Lewis, Outer Hebrides.

The Sun and the Seasons
A Celtic Cycle

TO ANY EARLY civilization the sun was the most important aspect of the natural world. The Incas of South America, along with many other cultures, formed an elaborate seasonal 'calendar', and on their sacred mountain of Macchu Picchu there is a standing stone called 'the tethering post of the sun'. On the shortest day of the year, a ritual ceremony took place there: a rope was tied to the stone and the sun god was invoked with a plea that the sun should go no lower in the sky but begin to return, bringing more light and warmth as the yearly cycle progressed into spring. Symbolically the sun was being 'tethered' and brought back.

In the Celtic world we have the festivals of the winter and summer solstices and the spring and autumn equinoxes. A popular misconception should be cleared up at the beginning. Though these festivals were observed by the Celts and their clear-seeing teachers, the druids, the origins of the festivals themselves are far more ancient and have their roots in the very earliest civilizations.

Ritual observance of these festivals at stone circles and standing stones, as well as a number of chambered cairns, which are all aligned in a certain way to the sun at these special times, goes back to the third millennium BC or even earlier. The tradition has been perpetuated, in places such as Ireland almost continuously, through the Celtic era.

The four 'quarter-festivals' which occur between the solstices and equinoxes in the yearly cycle are of Celtic origin. The Celtic New Year began on 1 November with the festival of Samhain. The veil between the worlds of spirit and matter was said at this time to be very thin, and the spirits of the ancestors could move freely between the two worlds. Today Hallowe'en (31 October) and All Saints' Day (1 November) are remnants of this most important festival.

The second of the four great Celtic festivals was Imbolc. This was celebrated on 1 February, between the winter solstice and the spring equinox. The festival coincided with the time that ewes began to give their milk. This was taken as an imminent sign of new birth and the end of winter. The festival was also directly connected with the goddess Brigit (subsequently St

Brigit), who was patroness of healing, divination, the arts and childbirth. It was said that many children were born around this time of the year, having been conceived during the fertile spring festival of Beltane.

Beltane was the third of the great Celtic festivals, celebrated on May Day, initiating the season of pollination and growth. Maypole dancing, a custom which continues today, is derived from this festival, and the original maypole was symbolic of the phallus and fertility. The literal meaning of Beltane is 'bright fire' and it also has associations with the sun god, Belenus. During this festival bonfires were lit on high places to reaffirm the return of the sun. Cattle were also driven between two fires as a purification ritual and to encourage their fertility.

Lughnasadh, on 1 August, was the time of the fourth great Celtic festival and season, that of abundance and harvest. The name is derived from Lugh in Irish mythology and Lleu in Welsh, meaning 'shining one'. Lugh was a widely revered deity in the Celtic world and his name is perpetuated in Luguvallium (Carlisle), Lugdunum (Lyons) and other place-names throughout Britain and Europe. The city of Lyons in France is home to the remains of the much debated Coligny Calendar. Bronze, dating from the first century BC, this is of a substantial size, measuring 5 by 3½ feet (1.5 x 1 m), and the fragments show a calendar of sixty-two lunar months plus two intercalary ones. The meaning of this calendar has not been fully established. Dark and light phases are indicated, as well as fortunate and unlucky days, which began at sunset and end at dusk. Roman numerals are used, yet the language is Gallic.

While still on the subject of Lugh, 'the shining one', it seems appropriate to mention the Tuatha Dé Danann, the people of the goddess Dana. In the early Irish sagas they were a race of supernatural beings who originally came from the sky, a beautiful and magical people with heroic leaders and powerful magicians, half gods and half men. In ancient Irish legend the Tuatha Dé Danann were said to have been the builders of the great chambered cairn at Newgrange, close to the River Boyne in County Meath. In the context of this chapter, it is well worth noting that the aperture above the passage entrance to the central chamber of Newgrange is exactly aligned with sunrise on the winter solstice. On this day only, the central chamber is illuminated; the womb of Mother Earth was impregnated with the rays of the sun, fertilizing the land with the spirit of new life. This chambered cairn, with its alignment, is one of the oldest buildings in the world and pre-dates the pyramids of Egypt by several hundred years. Recently the pyramids too

Opposite: *Lugh – the sun god.*

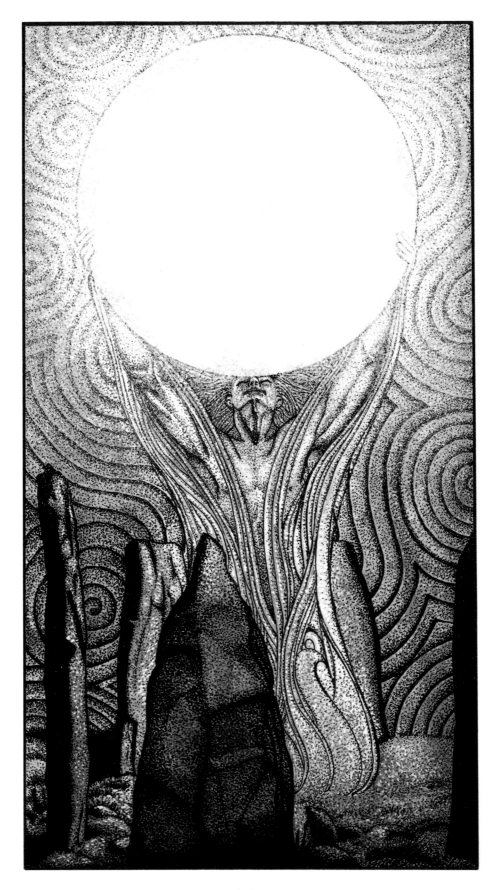

have been proved to have celestial alignment passages, not with the sun but with stellar constellations and the star Sirius.[15]

For the Celts, 3,000 years later, the Tuatha Dé Danann became the *sidhe*, the 'shining ones', Lords of Light, the 'gentry' or the fairy people, as mentioned in the previous chapter. These beings dwelt within the ancient mounds and hillforts, guarding the entrance to the Otherworld of eternal youth and never-ending joy. In Irish mythology the supreme chief of the Tuatha Dé Danann was Dagda, the all-knowing god of the sun.

There are various prehistoric sites associated with solar and planetary alignment. One of the best known must be Stonehenge in Wiltshire, where on the summer solstice the rising sun aligns with the 'heel stone'. There are also other planetary alignments connected with Stonehenge. At Callanish, on the Isle of Lewis in the Outer Hebrides, there stands probably the finest surviving example anywhere of a stone-circle complex. The stones form the shape of a vast ringed cross, with the arms orientated to the points of the compass. This circle has solar, lunar and planetary alignments, the entire structure being 400 feet (120 m) long and 150 feet (46 m) wide.

The ancient solstice and equinox festivals are echoed in today's calendar. The winter solstice has become Christmas or Yuletide, carrying its early associations with the sacred yew tree, and the yule (yew) log. The spring equinox has its reflection in today's Easter. The summer solstice has its counterpart in the Christian calendar with the feast of St John, and the autumn equinox is probably the least changed of the four, with its essence residing in the Christian harvest festival.

Likewise the substance of the four great Celtic festivals is preserved in today's Christian calendar. Samhain has its essence in All Souls' Day and All Saints' Day; Imbolc continues the tradition of Brigid as St Brigid's Day and Candlemas; Beltane coincides with the festival of Whitsun and Lughnasadh with that of Lammas.

Another interesting representation of the four Celtic festivals is as the Cosmic Family of father, mother, son and daughter.[16] At Lughnasadh the father is symbolized by Lugh, the sun god or 'shining one'. At Imbolc the mother is symbolized by Brigit, who presides over childbirth, and by Arianrhod, goddess of the moon, the feminine principle; her name literally means 'silver wheel'. At Beltane the son is symbolized by the sun god, Belanus; the 'tane' in the word Beltane comes from the early Welsh word '*tân*' meaning fire. At Samhain the daughter is symbolized by Caer and by Rhiannon. Caer Ibormeth appears in the early Irish sagas; her name is another association with the sacred yew tree, as it means 'yew berry'. She has the ability to change her shape and is able to turn into a white swan, a symbol of purity. Rhiannon is one of the key figures in the stories in the Welsh *Mabinogion*.

Entrance passage to Newgrange chambered cairn, County Meath, Ireland, c. 3200 BC.

To gain a clearer idea of the tremendous importance of the sun and the seasons to the Celts, we should try to envisage life on earth over 2,000 years ago. The cycles of the sun, the moon and the stars, with their effect on every aspect of the natural world, would have formed the organic basis for the structure of the Celtic year, with its seasonal festivals. This was, and still is, a way of life very much in harmony with our planet, and the ancient festivals are today being revived by an increasing number of people concerned with the earth's welfare.

Inherited Sites
A Legacy in Stone

THE LANDS in which tribes of Celtic origin finally settled had been occupied for thousands of years prior to their arrival. The earliest of these people were known as the megalith builders and the many chambered cairns that they built can be found mainly in coastal areas from southern Spain to Denmark. These chambered cairns date from 5000 BC onwards, and some are very accurately and elaborately constructed. It is uncertain whether they were actually used at a much later date by the incoming Celts, who must initially have been much in awe of them, due to their size and unusual appearance. We know that the druids were very familiar with astronomy, so it is more than likely that at least some of the major ones continued to be used for the ritual veneration of the Earth Mother.

There are many fine examples in today's Celtic countries, such as Bryn Celli Dhu on Anglesey, Maes Howe on the Orkney Isles and Newgrange in Ireland. The latter two have been accurately surveyed. The cairns consist of very large mounds built over a corbelled stone chamber with a passage to the outside. To give some idea of size, the mound at Newgrange is 340 feet (105 m) in diameter and 40 feet (12 m) high, and the passage to the central chamber is 60 feet (18 m) long. There is a stone circle surrounding the entire structure which originally consisted of thirty-nine invididual stones, and there are ninety-seven carved stones surrounding the cairn, providing some of the best examples of neolithic art to be found anywhere.

What is fascinating about many of these chambered cairns is that they were constructed so accurately that at sunrise on the winter solstice the sun shone right down the passageway and illuminated the central chamber, which at all other times of the year would have been in darkness. Both Newgrange and Maes Howe are examples of this type of construction. It is believed that this was directly connected with worship of the Earth Mother, which was widespread throughout Europe from as early as 30,000 BC. The purpose of the passage was to let the midwinter shaft of light enter the darkness of Mother Earth, ritually fertilizing Her and ensuring abundance for

Opposite: *Spirit of the Green Man.*

the coming year. Whether this occasion was presided over by a priest, or in much later days a druid, is not known, but it would seem likely as such importance was attached to this one-day event. It is easy to imagine the intense anticipation just before sunrise on the winter solstice in these places. When the golden orb of the sun appeared over the horizon, its rays would shine precisely down the passage, illuminating the central chamber and any symbolic carvings and ritual offerings within. The entire process was over in twenty minutes, and would not be repeated then for another year.

Newgrange dates from *c.* 3200 BC and Maes Howe from *c.* 2800 BC. Did the Celts and their teachers, the druids, later use these ceremonies? There is

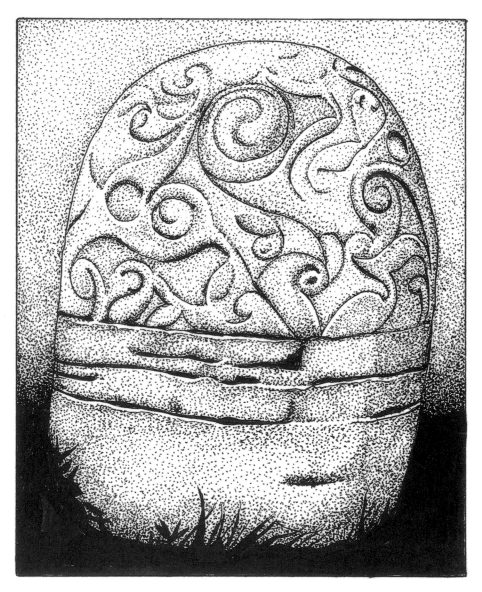

The Turoe Stone, County Galway, Ireland. This dates from between the third and the first century BC. The carvings possess strong similarities to La Tène designs.

The Burghead Bull. Pictish carving from eastern Scotland, seventh century AD.

*Trevethy Quoit, Cornwall. This consists of seven upright stones, about 10 ft high,
with a 12 ft-long capstone. This burial chamber dates from c. 4000 BC.*

no written record, but as the monuments are striking features in their lands,
it is necessary to mention them.

Dolmens – two or more standing stones with a large horizontal capstone
– are said to be monuments of this type, but the surrounding earthen chamber
has been eroded and washed away over thousands of years. The remaining
structure looks most imposing, and there are several well-known examples,
including Poulnabone dolmen on the Burran in County Clare, Ireland, and
Pentre Ifan in south-west Wales. The latter has a massive capstone estimated
to weigh over 40 tons, supported by several sturdy, upright stones. The site
is magnificent, being on a hillside overlooking the Preselli mountains in the
heart of this Celtic land. It is hard to think that over 3,000 years later
seasonal observances, as well as ancestor worship, were not being carried
out here by the Celts of the region.

'Guardian of Callanish'. The standing stones of Callanish, Isle of Lewis, Outer Hebrides.

'St Brigid'.

Stone circles exist in abundance in the Celtic countries. Again we have no direct evidence that they were used by the Celts, but because many of them have solar or lunar alignments, and the druids were known for their knowledge of astronomy, it seems highly likely that they would have been. These stone circles are of a later date than the chambered cairns. The earliest date from around 2800 BC, though most examples are considerably later than this. The alignments of Stonehenge and Callanish are discussed briefly in the previous chapter.

'The Swan Maiden'.

Another type of megalithic layout was the stone row or 'avenue'. Examples of these are found at Carnac in Brittany, West Kennet, near Avebury in Wiltshire, and Shovel Down on Dartmoor in Devon. As well as being carefully aligned, these stone avenues are said to have been used for processional rituals during the ancient festival days. The avenues at Carnac are the most spectacular and by far the largest. Fortunately, in the last few years almost the whole area has been fenced off from the public to allow natural vegetation to grow again. Due to the large number of visitors every year, the surrounding shrubs were being destroyed, which in turn was starting to affect the foundations of some of the stones.

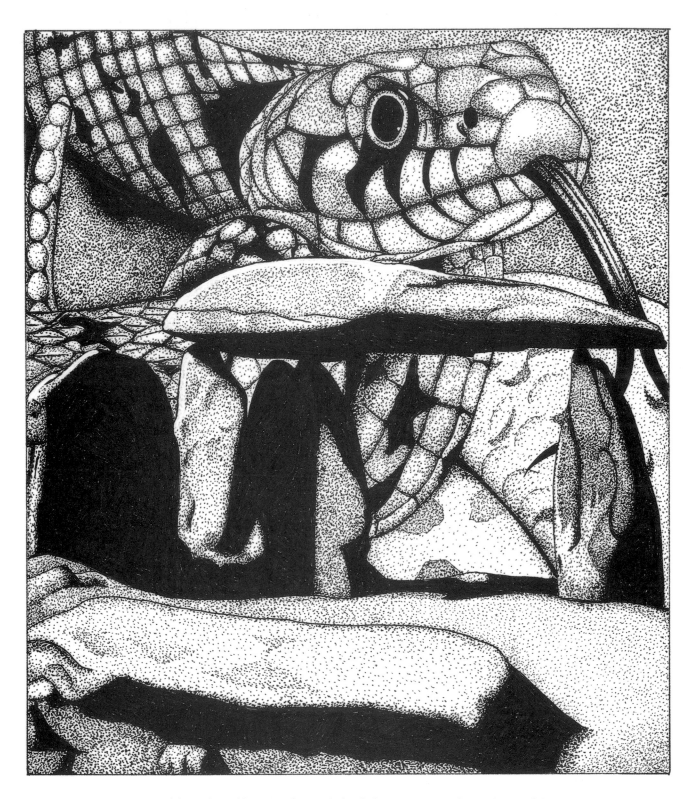

'*Serpent of the Underworld*'. *Pentre Ifan cromlech, which was once covered in earth, in Dyfed, Wales.*
The capstone weighs over 40 tons. The cromlech dates from c. 4000 BC.

The Ogham Stone from Ivybridge, Devon, which is now in the British Museum; sixth century AD. This also has a Latin inscription.

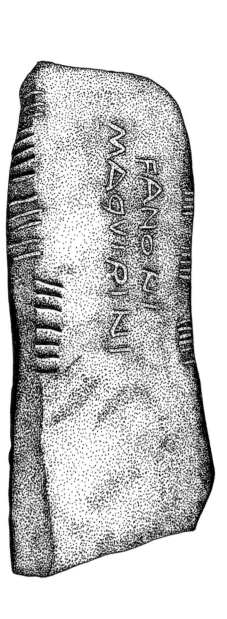

Single standing stones also exist in profusion throughout the Celtic countries. Some were erected as markers of ancient sacred sites, while a few have been found to align with the sunrise, sunset or the moon over a distant mountain on one of the festival days. At this point we can mention ogham script, the early Irish alphabet. Standing stones, some of which had been erected in prehistoric times, were carved with ogham inscriptions by the Celts. These stones can be found widely in Ireland, and also in areas of early Irish influence such as western Scotland and west Wales. Most of the inscriptions relate to particular chieftains and date from the third to the seventh century AD. An Irish manuscript, the Book of Ballymote, written in the fourteenth century, contains a detailed account of ogham and the relationship of the characters to the natural world, trees, rivers and types of food.

Ogham itself consists of a series of cuts or strokes made along a straight line positioned vertically. Individual letters have their specific strokes to the left or the right side of the line. There are approximately 400 known ogham stones, including several in Cornwall and the Isle of Man. One of the most interesting is the Maglocunus Stone, which is today found within Nevern church in Dyfed. This stone, which presumably once stood upright in the area, has an ogham inscription with a Latin translation carved on the same face. It was this stone that gave the key to the understanding of ogham.

Other mysterious stones were left by earlier civilizations as legacies to the incoming Celts. Whether they were avoided, perhaps because of superstition or their strange designs, or whether they were familiar to them and incorporated into their belief system, is not known. A further example is the 'cup and ring' carvings found in northern Britain, Ireland and Wales, as well as in Europe. Some of these carvings are said to date from as early as 3400 BC. A fine accessible example is the Badger Stone on Ilkley Moor in north Yorkshire.

'Beehive' cells and an early Celtic cross, Skellig Michael, County Kerry, Ireland. This is probably the most remote and well-preserved early Celtic monastic settlement and is sited on a ledge 600 ft (180 metres) up on a small conical island seven miles (11 km) off the Kerry coast.

The Monastic Tradition
Celtic Christianity

WE DO NOT know exactly when Christianity first came to Britain but legends, which often contain a surprising amount of truth, even if they seem unlikely in later years, say that Joseph of Arimathea founded the first Christian church in Glastonbury in the first century AD. Joseph is said to have planted his staff in the ground close to the place where he wished to build his church. This grew and blossomed into what is now known as the Glastonbury Thorn. He is also depicted in a stained-glass window in today's church in the town.

There are also legends suggesting that Jesus himself visited Cornwall. This is not beyond the bounds of possibility, taking into account the tin-trading route in existence then. This ran between Phoenicia and Cornwall, the latter being at one time the largest tin-producing country in the western world.

There is no doubt that Celtic Christianity started in Ireland and from there spread very widely. St Patrick is said to have founded the Celtic Church of Ireland in AD 432, but it was almost certainly in existence well before this. Patrick himself, in later writings, is said to have been born in western Britain and at an early age been captured by pirates, who took him across to Ireland. He eventually returned to the mainland and, after travelling to Auxerre to receive religious instruction, returned much later as a missionary to Ireland.

Interesting and plausible links have been made between the early Coptic Church of Egypt and Ireland;[17] this is a subject that deserves more research. On the Drosten Stone in western Scotland there is an inscription in ogham alongside another in Greek. This stone dates from the sixth century AD, indicating that monks with a knowledge of the Greek language were already in this area and that the original Celtic Christianity had its roots in the Near East, rather than coming to Britain via Europe and the Roman Church.

The earliest recorded monastic community is that of St Ninian at Whithorn in Galloway, south-west Scotland. It was known as Candida Casa, the White House, and was founded in AD 397.

The whole essence of Celtic Christianity was very different to the Christianity of today. As well as being instructed by their teachers to travel to the remotest parts of the earth, the Celtic monks felt a strong compulsion to explore the unknown. This may well have been inherited from their itinerant ancestors, described earlier in this book. There was much synthesis between pagan beliefs and the early Christian Church. A number of churches were founded close to oak groves, in respect of the sanctity of the trees. As already mentioned, Kildare (Cille Daire) means 'church of the oaks'; there are various other examples. For the early monks a building was not seen as an essential. All of nature contained divinity, and was venerated as such. There is a wonderful Welsh word 'hud'; these three letters may be literally translated as 'a sense of wonder at the divine residing in everything'. 'Hud' expresses the essence of the early Celtic Church.

Sexual equality was totally observed and there are numerous female Celtic saints. This is hardly surprising as their predecessors had worshipped Mother Earth and the Goddess over a period of approximately 30,000 years! Marriage within the priesthood was quite acceptable, and there are records of a number of Celtic saints having wives, including St Brynach of Wales, of whom a contemporary biography still exists.

This reverence for all living things, or 'green spirituality' as we would call it today, is very much reflected in the association of animals with the Celtic saints and hermits. Birds especially were befriended, as they were thought to be intermediaries between this and a higher world. Specific birds, such as the owl, the eagle and the dove, were held to possess oracular powers and in various legends are said to have communicated with the saints.

The sixth century AD saw the flowering of the Celtic monastic system, and there followed one of the most creative periods in the world's history. This included the designing of the great illuminated Gospels of Kells, Durrow, Lindisfarne and other less well-known manuscripts. It also included the golden era of Celtic metalwork mentioned in an earlier chapter. The Celtic monasteries were an ideal setting for this creativity to flourish, being places of peace and tranquillity, meditation and contemplation, where any sense of urgency or haste for creative ventures was absent. Also during this era the great Celtic high crosses were carved and erected. From careful analysis, many scholars believe that the high crosses were originally painted in bright colours, highlighting the scriptural scenes which are carved on them.[18] In view of the vibrant colours used in the great Gospels, this would seem highly likely. These crosses are found in Ireland, western Scotland, south-west Wales and Cornwall.

Opposite: A round tower, Clonmacnoise, County Offaly, Ireland. Tenth century AD.

There are over forty major monastic sites in Ireland from this period, an early example being at Clonmacnoise, close to the River Shannon. This was founded by St Ciaran in AD 545 as a place of teaching, with a subsequent exodus of monks and nuns from there to many distant lands. The methods of oral teaching and story-telling and the incorporation of all aspects of the natural world reflect a strong continuance of many elements of the earlier druidic tradition. Major monastic sites in Ireland include St Brigid's monastery at Kildare and St Kevin's monastery at Glendalough, with its spectacular little oratory known as St Kevin's kitchen still standing today. Also St Finian's monastery at Clonard, where the young St Columba studied before founding his own monastery at Derry, in an oak grove which had previously been a sacred druidic site. It was after this that he was exiled from Ireland and founded the monastery on Iona. During the sixth century AD St David founded his monastery at Menevia in south-west Wales. St David's mother was St Non, a widely travelled Celtic nun whose original ruined chapel, with its very early slab cross, can be visited today. It is situated close to the cliff edge on the most westerly coast of Dyfed, and the sixth-century-AD chapel was built within a prehistoric stone circle, the remains of which is still visible. This site must surely be seen as the perpetuation of belief systems with a very similar basis. Both St Non and St David travelled widely; together they went to Brittany, and St David is said to have made a pilgrimage to Jerusalem – no mean feat in those days!

St Columcille, or Columba, was also an Irish monk at this period. Due to confrontations with the king of Ireland over the copying of sacred manuscripts, Columba was banished from the country and set sail into the unknown with twelve of his followers. His orders were that they were to travel until they reached land from which Ireland was not visible. Apparently they first landed on the Mull of Kintyre, but on looking westward they could still see Ireland. They dutifully continued until eventually reaching the island of Iona, in the Inner Hebrides. It is documented that they landed here in the year AD 563. Living on the island at the time was a druid named Oran, whom Columba befriended. Columba founded the original monastery on Iona. The sixth-century-AD chapel of Oran, who later became St Oran, still stands there today, close to the rebuilt abbey buildings. Iona was, and still is, one of the wonders of the Celtic world. It is known today as the Mecca of the Gael. It is believed that the Book of Kells was created here by Irish monks. The reason it was known as the Book of Kells is that the first written record of its existence, just after 1000, states that it was in use in the church of Kells, County Meath. It is likely that it was brought across to Ireland by monks fleeing from one of the fierce Viking raids on

Iona. It was stolen from Kells church and subsequently recovered after 'twenty nights and two months' of being 'buried under a sod', with its binding of gold and precious stones missing. If this story is correct, taking into account the Irish weather, it certainly says a lot about the high quality of ink and colour pigments used by the Celtic monks! Today the original book resides in the library of Trinity College, Dublin, from where colour slides of some of the most magnificent pages can be obtained. The Book of Kells is said to be one of the most beautiful works of art ever created.

The sanctity of Iona was such that kings and queens of Scotland, Ireland and even Scandinavia and France requested to be buried there in an ancient cemetery known as 'the burial place of the kings'. Beehive cells, tiny stone-built hermitages just large enough for one person, were often constructed by the Celtic monks as places for retreat and solitude. The remains of St Columba's beehive cell can still be seen on Iona. Also on the island are two superb early Celtic high crosses, of St John and St Martin, dating from the eighth and ninth centuries AD, as well as other Celtic monuments.

Lindisfarne Priory ruins. The original Celtic monastery of St Aidan, who came from Iona, was destroyed by Viking raids between AD 793 and 875. The present-day ruins are c.1100.

An indication of the spiritual energy grounded there by the early Celtic monks is given by the fact that Iona is still today one of the most important places of pilgrimage in the Western hemisphere. Set like a tiny jewel in a sapphire-blue sea, it is visited by many thousands of pilgrims every year.

There was one major danger to the Celtic monasteries and that was invasion by the Vikings. These people were very experienced boatmen and would attack using the element of surprise, pillaging and killing anyone who resisted. They travelled long distances, laying siege to many of the Scottish islands, coastal areas of Ireland, the Isle of Man and north-west Britain, including Lindisfarne, and later, in the ninth and tenth centuries AD, Holland, France, the Brittany coast and even the northern and southern coasts of Spain. It became known that monasteries contained wealth in the form of valuable gold and silver religious artefacts, as well as the great Gospels, with their jewel-encrusted gold bindings. Thus the Celtic monks were aware that at any point they were in danger of a surprise attack.

In Ireland an effective way of protection was to build round towers. Each major monastic site had its round tower, a feature of the landscape unique to Ireland. Their construction was extremely solid and the shape was rather similar to a pencil – tall and slim, with a conical roof. It is hardly surprising that some medieval historians misinterpreted them as being phallic symbols associated with fertility rites!

Their true function was to provide a place of refuge for the monks in times of attack. The tallest round tower, part of which still stands at Clonmacnoise, was originally over 100 feet (30 m) high, and a number of others approach this height. The single doorways were at least 6 feet (2 m) from the ground and were reached using a wooden ladder which was hauled back inside after the last person had entered the tower. As some monasteries were plundered several times during their history, these round towers must have some fascinating tales to tell, and must have been the saving grace of many religious artefacts and manuscripts, as well as concealing the monks themselves. It is a pity that for some reason Iona did not build one. Perhaps the tiny island was not able to provide the materials for its construction, or the Atlantic gales were too severe. Consequently, under Viking attack the library there, which was reputed to have the largest collection of ecclesiastical books in Europe, was completely destroyed. It is a sobering thought to imagine how many other illuminated manuscripts similar to the surviving great gospels were needlessly destroyed.

An earlier Scottish equivalent to the round tower, though fewer were built, was the broch, a much lower and wider circular stone structure. Although it provided some protection, invaders would have found it easier

'Spirit of Iona'. St Martin's Cross, Iona, western Scotland; late eighth century AD.

to scale and enter. Examples of brochs survive in the Western Isles, on the Isle of Skye and on the Scottish mainland.

While on the subject of Celtic monasteries, it is interesting to describe the most unusual example of all. The Celtic monks and hermits were dedicated to finding remote places in which to carry out their devotions. Many cells and chapels exist in very isolated surroundings, and it seems likely that the choice of place was influenced by the monks' predecessors of the pagan world. Locations by streams or wells, in forests, especially oak groves, in caves and on islands – all of these are not uncommon. But the monastery that stands out as being by far the most extreme is that on Skellig Michael, County Kerry.

Out in the Atlantic ocean, between 7 and 9 miles (11 and 14 km) off the very south-western tip of Ireland lie the Skellig Islands. Little Skellig is now a bird sanctuary. The furthest away, Greater Skellig or Skellig Michael, was a Celtic monastic community from about AD 625 until AD 875. The island is a small, dark cone of granite rising straight out of the sea. The eastward side mainly has a slope of 60 degrees to the horizontal, while most of the side facing the Atlantic is sheer, and the tiny island rises to a pinnacle of 700 feet (215 m). It is accessible only on calm days, as landing is a case of 'jump when you can' on to the nearest ledge. There are no beaches or places to draw up a boat and there is only one tiny inlet for a small craft to enter. There are no trees or shrubs here, and apart from a small modern lighthouse no life save seabirds and a few rabbits. Perched about 600 feet (185 m) up on a ledge there is a meticulously constructed dry-stone enclosure with seven beehive cells built by early Celtic monks. Within this enclosure there is a small section known as the Monks' Garden. It is believed that the monks actually brought fertile earth from the mainland, as none exists here. There is a rough-hewn cross, carved from a single large granite boulder, and two small chapels or oratories, as well as a small burial ground within a stone enclosure. Surprisingly, there is a fresh water well on this ledge.

At a cursory glance, anyone today would imagine that one night on the island would be a reasonably alarming experience, exposed to the full force of the Atlantic storms on this jagged granite cone devoid of vegetation and with near-vertical cliffs. Yet as an indication of the austerity of a few of the more extreme Celtic monks, this island was inhabited for over 250 years! It might have been possible for a goat to live on the island, providing milk and cheese, and the well would have provided fresh water. Apart from the meagre vegetables grown in the Monks' Garden (if they ever managed to survive the gales), fish and seabird eggs would have been the only other sources of food. Perched on their tiny eyrie far above the crashing ocean, these monks did survive here until AD 875, when they were invaded by the Vikings. Their bishop was barbarically killed by being starved to death, and the few remaining monks who managed to hide in remote crevices on the island soon found that the Vikings had destroyed their small coracles. Being unable to return to the mainland, they eventually also starved to death, and the island has subsequently remained uninhabited.

A Christian penance, and it is hard to imagine anything more extreme, was inaugurated here in the Middle Ages. This took the form of setting out from the Irish mainland, landing on the island (if the weather made this feasible) and then climbing what is known as the Way of the Cross, which is a hazardous series of slippery steps carved into the rock face by the early monks. This path, apart from its near-vertical incline in many places and slippery winding steps, ascends to the very summit of the conical island. At this point the unfortunate repentant was obliged to slide out along an outcrop of rock, suspended over the raging ocean 700 feet (215 m) below, and kiss the cross which is carved into the end of the projecting stone. It is hard to imagine the kind of unseemingly act which could merit such a dramatic penance!

The inherent longing of the Celtic monks to venture into the unknown has already been mentioned. The actual distances that many of them travelled are by today's standards remarkable. Many people will have read Tim Severin's captivating book which indicates that the Irish monks were capable of sailing from their own country as far as the North American continent.[19]

During the sixth century AD there was a massive exodus of monks and nuns who had trained in the Irish monasteries. Some chose the path of solitude and built small hermitages on remote islands or in inaccessible locations in the countries where they landed. There were three main routes of travel. The first was across to mainland Britain, where chapels and larger monastic communities were founded. Northern Scotland, the Isle of Man, north and south Wales, Northumbria, Cornwall and the south-west of Britain all received an influx of Irish monks and nuns, and many of the tiny chapels they built still remain today, as do holy wells and carved crosses which bear their names. The Celtic saints are also remembered in various place-names in these areas. For example, Perranporth in Cornwall is 'the port of St Piran'.

The other two routes were initiated and fostered by two key figures of the Irish Celtic Church, St Columba and St Columbanus. These two were contemporaries, Columbanus being a few years younger than Columba. He was born in AD 543 and would have been twenty years old when Columba landed on Iona.

Columba's monks and, after his death in AD 597, his followers set out from Iona, travelling through Scotland and northern Britain, eventually founding several large monasteries, including the famous one on the holy island of Lindisfarne, off the east coast of Northumbria, in AD 635. They travelled as far south as East Anglia and the kingdom of Mercia, teaching and building small chapels where individual monks remained. Their demise began with the Synod of Whitby in AD 664, when the Roman Church, which had recently arrived in Britain, challenged some of the main tenets of Celtic Christianity. Due to the might of Rome, dates of major Celtic Christian festivals and other customs were changed at this major religious meeting, and Celtic Christianity declined rapidly from then onwards. Fortunately nowadays, 1,300 years later, people are seeing the wisdom of the early Celtic Church. Its essence, along with many of its beliefs and customs, have started a revival of 'green spirituality' which is beginning to re-energize and bring alive much of the arid dogma of today's 'Churchianity'.

The travels and adventures of the monk Columbanus and his followers provide the third avenue for the spread of the Irish Celtic Church. Like St Columba, he set out with twelve followers, landing in Gaul and travelling very extensively on the Continent. One surprising recorded fact is that he was fifty-seven years old when he initially set out on his missionary works. Travelling through Frankish lands, he founded several monasteries, including one at Luxeuil which was on the site of a derelict Roman fort. He and his followers travelled on to Lake Constance, in what is now Switzerland, where they met with so much hostility that they retreated from that region. After a number of years of further travelling and teaching, he founded his last monastery at Bobbio in the Apennines, at the age of seventy. The Celtic monks were certainly renowned for their stamina!

His descendants travelled even more widely, though by then the pure strain of the Celtic Church had started to come under the influence of the Church of Rome and its values had been modified accordingly.

Taking into account the vast areas travelled by the Irish monks, it is no surprise to find the beautiful Celtic art form which they carried with them appearing in a number of early European illuminated Church manuscripts, such as the Gospels of Echternach and Maaseik, the Trier Gospels, the St Martin-des-Champs Gospels, the Barberini Gospels (now in the Vatican) and the Montpelier Psalter. Most of these are early to mid-eighth century AD, and all contain fine examples of Celtic-influenced artwork.

The Leningrad Gospels is the manuscript located the furthest distance from Ireland, the home of the great illuminated Gospels. This is a beautiful late eighth-century-AD Northumbrian-Celtic manuscript now residing in the library of St Petersburg (a much more appropriate name for the city) in Russia. Whether the Celtic monks actually travelled as far as Russia is not known, but it is more likely that the manuscript found its way there at a later date, possibly as a royal gift.

This chapter has given some insight into the widespread influence of the early Celtic Church, and also its magnificent artwork, which has been so much admired over the centuries.

A Celtic cross at Kilfenora, County Clare, Ireland, depicting a monk with a book-satchel. Twelfth century AD.

Glorious Carvings
The Celtic Cross

To the many people interested in Celtic culture, the Celtic cross is probably one of the most familiar images. Otherwise known as the wheel cross, this symbol in its various stages of development spans over 1,000 years, from approximately AD 300 to AD 1400. There are also a few fine contemporary examples, as well as some inferior Victorian 'imitations', to be found in churchyards throughout Britain and Ireland.

From the outset, it should be pointed out that the function of the early Celtic cross was as a carving 'to the greater glory of God' and not, except in a very few cases, as a gravestone or burial marker. The free-standing Celtic cross was a monument to the divine in all things, a meeting place for worship and also a focal point for travelling pilgrims and lay folk.

The development of the Celtic cross is fascinating. The very earliest examples are found as plain, mainly uncircled crosses carved on to standing stones. Some of these carvings may be fourth century AD or even slightly earlier. Two schools of thought exist as to why the crosses were carved on these stones. The first is the more puritan idea that the stones, being pagan in their origin, needed 'Christianizing' as they did not fit into the belief system of the early Christian Celts.

The second is rather the opposite, that pagan places of worship were held in esteem by the early Celtic church (as has been seen by the siting of a number of monasteries close to oak groves, for example), and the addition of a Christian cross to the standing stone was a mark of respect and the continuance and evolution of an already existing tradition of worship.

Some intriguing early examples exist. One at Aglish in County Kerry is a standing stone, itself of uncertain age. The two angular sides have ogham inscriptions carved on them, and at the top of the flat portion there is a 'Greek' equal-armed cross, with its arms tapering towards the centre. The cross is surrounded by an unbroken circle. It may be possible to view this stone as a blending of pagan, Christian and early Irish cultures.

St Columba's cave near Ellary, Argyll, is another place the writer has been fortunate enough to visit. In its beautiful and remote setting, close to an early ruined Celtic chapel and beside a small sea loch, it contains a very basic stone altar built from many small, flat stones. Above this, and carved into the rock face, are a number of small, plain crosses of a very early date. The cave, with its inner chamber, is said at one time to have been a refuge for St Columba from the invading Vikings.

Following on from the crosses carved into standing stones, marker stones and rock faces, we have the very basic and powerful early slab crosses. Good examples of these exist in all the Celtic countries. Most of them were carved on to a flat, roughly oblong stone, and the symbol is a plain equal-armed cross like a plus sign, surrounded by a circle. Occasionally the lower arm of the cross extends below the circle. Two examples of this style are in St Non's chapel in Dyfed and Kilmory chapel, Knapdale, Argyll. Often the spaces between the equal arms of the encircled cross were deeply indented, an indication of the evolution at a later date into the tall, free-standing crosses with fully hollowed circles.

As slab crosses evolved, the designs became a little more elaborate: for instance, the cross design being formed from a single interlacing line. There is an example of this type on a solid stone, also with an ogham inscription, at Dugoed in Wales. Occasionally at an even later date Latin inscriptions were added to the same stones, commemorating important regional chiefs or rulers. In the seventh and eighth centuries AD some of the slab crosses are found with ornate and complex Celtic designs carved on them. A fine example is to be found in Tullylease churchyard, County Cork, dating from the eighth century AD. It also has the name Berechtuine carved beside the design.

Another very unusual type of early Celtic cross has a carving of the human head at the top, with the side-arms of the cross formed into spirals representing actual arms and the longer shaft either tapering into primitive feet or, as in one example originally from Riskbuie in Argyll, forming a fish, the symbol of Christianity. There is a very early and basically carved example of this style of cross in Nevern church, Dyfed, probably of sixth-century-AD origin.

The blossoming of the slab cross into the most spectacular stone carvings occurs in the Pictish regions of northern and eastern Scotland. Pictish art is a subject in its own right;[20] later examples of these carvings are Celtic-influenced and employ a combination of highly elaborate knotwork and spiral designs, together with the Pictish love of animal and bird designs, as well as mysterious symbols. In the year AD 843 the Scottish and Pictish kingdoms were united, which would have increased the artistic exchange between the two cultures. Early this century J. Romilly Allen[21] placed these stones into three categories. Class I stones contain purely Pictish symbols, the main date of these being the seventh century AD. Class II stones, which

'High Cross'. The Cross of Muirdeach, Monasterboice, County Louth, Ireland. This is probably the finest and most intricately carved of the Irish high crosses. Ninth century AD.

contain elaborate knotwork Celtic crosses surrounded by Pictish carvings, are considered to date from the mid-eighth to the mid-ninth centuries. The Class III stones were those in this region which were devoid of Pictish symbols and consisted solely of intricately carved Celtic crosses and designs. These slab crosses Romilly Allen dated from the mid-ninth century AD onwards. Many of them are decorated on both sides.

Examples of each of these types of cross should be mentioned, although Class I stones do not have a Celtic influence and are strictly Pictish in design, possessing their own intrinsic beauty and mystery. Among the Class I carvings the image of a bull is found at Burghead, and a beautifully stylized wild boar carving comes from Knocknagael. Mysterious symbols such as crescents, V and Z rods and discs, as well as sea horses and eagles, are also found on this class of stone. Other examples are the Rhynie Man stone and the symbol-carved stone at Dunnichen, the top design on which has been said to represent stylized flowers and leaves.

Moving on to the Class II stones, some truly magnificent examples exist, with highly elaborate and complex knotwork crosses, possibly influenced by the designs in the great Gospels. Surrounding the crosses are figures of warriors on horseback, animals, mythical beasts and occasionally Pictish symbols. Many of these slab crosses are decorated on both sides. Noteworthy examples are from Rossie Priory, Shandwick in Ross-shire, Glamis churchyard, St Madoes and Meigle in Perthshire, Kirriemuir, Inchbraoch and Aberlemno in Angus-shire. The front of the latter free-standing stone is composed of a very elaborate knotwork cross surrounded by mythical beasts and a pair of sea horses. There is a fascinating example in Elgin Cathedral, Morayshire. The cross was discovered during road repairs in 1828 and subsequently taken to the cathedral. The front depicts a Celtic cross with intricate interlacing, now very worn, and is surrounded by carvings of the four Evangelists. Beneath the cross design are intertwined birds. The reverse of the slab consists of Pictish designs. There is a double disc and a Z rod, and a crescent decorated with spirals. Beneath this is carved a hunting scene with riders on horseback, a stag, birds and hunting dogs.

A good example of Class III is the Farr Stone from Sutherland. This free-standing slab cross in a small churchyard is truly magnificent, consisting of a Celtic cross with a triple spiral as its centre, a knotwork wheel and fret-pattern upper arms. Above and beneath the cross, the stone is filled with rectangles of elaborate key-patterning. The cross design itself has a chalice-type knotwork base within which are carved two birds with necks intertwined. The entire area of the free-standing slab is filled with intricate designwork and the overall effect is most beautiful. The cross probably dates from the mid-ninth century AD and is in a very good state of preservation.

Further west, in Ireland, western Scotland, Wales, the Isle of Man and Cornwall, the slab cross evolved into the great high crosses of the eighth–tenth centuries AD. These are probably the best known of all the Celtic crosses. The style in each Celtic country differs slightly, so it is best to describe typical examples from each.

Ireland was probably the home of the high cross, and wonderful examples can be seen in association with early monastic sites. These crosses were known as Scripture crosses, as the scenes carved on the faces and sides depict biblical events. The major sites include Clonmacnoise, Monasterboice, Moone, Kells, Castledermot, Duleek, Ahenny and Durrow.

The high cross at Monasterboice, County Louth, is a splendid one and will serve as an example. On its base is an Irish inscription which reads: 'A prayer for Muiredach, for whom this cross was made.' Muiredach was an abbot there who died *c*. AD 922. The cross is about 10 feet (3 m) in height and is set into a tapered base. The wheel of the cross is delicate and fully perforated. The top arm tapers into an elaborately carved 'roof' shape. Explanations for this vary, ranging from the mundane idea that this shape

An early slab cross from Clonmacnoise, County Offaly, Ireland. Probably eighth century AD.

deflected the rain and thus prevented the monument eroding, to the roof being symbolic of the 'House of God'. As with all these high crosses, both faces are elaborately carved and there is a crucifixion scene at the centre. The sides, base and wheel are also profusely carved with knotwork and key-pattern designs. Many of these crosses now stand in churchyards alongside monuments and carvings of a much later date. When originally erected, they would have stood on their own and provided a strikingly beautiful and awe-inspiring meeting place for the Celtic monks. It is also believed that they were originally painted in bright colours, similar to those used in the great Gospels. If this was the case, they would have been truly wonderful to behold. Today, over 1,000 years later, they are still some of the most beautiful and intricate stone sculptures in the western hemisphere.

In Wales there are several free-standing high crosses of this era. The finest are those at Carew and Nevern, both in Dyfed, and Maen Achwyfan, near Whitford in Clwyd. A description of the Nevern cross will serve as an example.

Nevern is possibly one of the most concentrated of Celtic sites anywhere. It has an avenue of very ancient yew trees in the churchyard and two ogham stones. It has a very early slab cross and beyond the churchyard there is a holy well. It was also a marker point on the old Pilgrims' Route from Canterbury to St David's Cathedral. But its pride and glory is the Nevern great cross, which stands only a few feet from the church wall. The cross is about 13 feet (4 m) high and of very solid proportions. Unlike the Irish high crosses, it has no open-spaced wheel but a solid head made in a separate section and carefully joined. This head is small and circular, with basic Celtic interlacing picking out the cross design on it, interspersed with four raised bosses. The designs on the very solid shaft are basic knotwork and key patterns, as well as angular decoration that is said by some to be of Scandinavian influence. This is a wondrous giant of a cross, and to be in its vicinity is to experience a sense of solidity and power. It is said to date from the late tenth or early eleventh century.

In Scotland there are a few fine examples from the high cross era. Some of the better known are the Kildalton cross on the Isle of Islay, St John's cross and St Martin's cross on Iona, and the Kilmartin cross, Argyll, though the latter may be of a slightly earlier date.

St John's cross on Iona and the Kildalton cross on Islay bear a striking resemblance to each other, and may well have been carved by the same school of stoneworkers, known as the Iona school. They have a beauty and delicacy all of their own, being thinner than the Irish and Welsh high crosses, with a wider, more slender wheel. The Kildalton cross has biblical figures carved on the arms and delicate knotwork on the slender wheel. Towards the base of the shaft is an elaborate patterning of spirals and bosses, while at the very centre of the cross is a 'bird's-nest' design, this being a raised boss with a central indentation. The cross stands almost 9 feet (2.75 m) high and, along with St John's cross on Iona, is dated to the latter half of the eighth century AD.

Two notable examples of free-standing Celtic crosses in Cornwall of this era are at Cardinham and Lanherne. The latter has been moved from its original location. Both of these have fully hollowed wheel heads, and are rather smaller than the crosses in the previously mentioned Celtic countries. They are of stocky proportions, the wheel head being compacted into the shaft. At Cardinham the cross within the wheel contains symmetrical Celtic knotwork, and the shaft has 'ring-chain' ornament which is of Scandinavian influence. The Lanherne cross has a crucifixion carving in relief, beneath which is a panel of broad Celtic knotwork. Near to the base is the name Runhol, probably the sculptor. These crosses are said to date from the ninth century AD.

The Isle of Man contains various examples of early Celtic slab crosses. However, due to Viking occupation, which commenced soon after the first invasions in AD 798, the main crosses on the island are a blend of Celtic and Scandinavian art.[22] They employ the Celtic wheel cross as a basis, surrounded with ring-chain designs and carvings depicting scenes from the Norse sagas. There are a few notable exceptions, one being at Lonan. This cross is considerably smaller than any of those previously mentioned and has a disproportionately large disc head incorporating a Celtic knotwork design of very elaborate knotwork, surrounded by a knotwork wheel. Though this cross dates from the ninth century AD, it is purely Celtic in design. There are two Welsh crosses of similar style and date in Margam Abbey museum, in west Glamorgan.

The last style of Celtic cross dates from the eleventh to the fourteenth centuries. It is distinctive from its predecessors in being very slender and having a small disc head without openings. The outlines of these crosses are mostly very even and symmetrical, and often less than 6 inches (15 cm) thick. A foliate patterning is often used down the thin sides, and the head has a crucifixion sculpture carved in high relief. The shafts and often the reverse have very elaborate Celtic knotwork ornamentation and foliate patterning. In Scotland fine examples exist at Oronsay Priory, Campbeltown, Argyll (c. 1380), on Iona (MacLean's cross) and, more stylized, at Kilmory, where the cross has carvings of a deer and a sword on the shaft.

Examples of this era and style are to be found throughout Ireland at various sites, including Cashel, Dysert O'Dea, Glendalough, Roscrea, Kilfenora and the Aran Islands.

There are very few Welsh examples of this late style of Celtic cross, but the head of one can be seen at Llangan, in south Glamorgan. Late Celtic crosses of this type are absent from Cornwall and the Isle of Man.

So, the styles of Celtic crosses are obviously many and varied. For the lover of fine-quality stone carvings, there are numerous sites in magnificent locations waiting to be visited, admired and respected.

EARLY IRISH CARVINGS

While on the topic of Celtic stone carvings, there is a small group which, due to its very early and unusual nature, should not be omitted. They are to be found in the lower Lough Erne area of County Fermanagh, Northern Ireland. Lower Lough Erne is close to the north-west coast and, although almost 2 miles (3 km) inland, is joined to the sea by a stretch of river, bridged at Ballyshannon. The lough has many small islands, the largest being Boa Island.

The main feature of these carvings is the human face, and the style is unique in Celtic stone figures. Their date varies according to different texts. Some place them as late as the seventh century AD, while others believe they are among the earliest Irish carvings of the first millennium AD. The latter would seem to be much more likely, as they are a combination of pagan and early monastic design.

The carvings are found at three sites: Boa Island, White Island and Killadeas, which is on the south-eastern shore of the lough.

The figures, and there are two of them on Boa Island, are known as Lustyman 1 and Lustyman 2 (the reason for their name is that they originally stood on Lustymore Island, just off the main island). The carvings are very similar in design, though Lustyman 2 is the best preserved. It consists of two male, robed figures back to back, with large heads with long, pointed chins. The nearest similar-shaped heads occur in early manuscripts from the Near East, and this could point to a link between the Coptic Church and Ireland. Between the two heads the stone is hollowed out, providing a receptacle for offerings or perhaps holy water. Their style is so unlike that of any of the early monastic carvings that it is quite likely they were left *in situ* by the monks, who may well have seen them as having mysterious pagan origins.

On White Island, when the Board of Works came to restore the early chapel on the island in 1928, they found six carvings actually embedded in the chapel wall, and another two were discovered buried in the churchyard. It is not known exactly why, but these figures seem to have been deliberately hidden.

Possibly their design portrayed too much of an early pagan influence for them to be accepted by Celtic monks. The carvings have an ancient Celtic beauty all of their own and are now exposed for the traveller to view.

In the churchyard at Killadeas, there is a carving known as the Bishop's Stone. On this stocky stone is carved a priest with crozier and bell, while the front again is dominated by the figure of a head with pointed chin. It is possible that the designs on this stone were carved at different dates.

This small group of carvings around lower Lough Erne is unique, and adds to the mystery of that fascinating time when the belief systems of the original Irish inhabitants and the early Celtic monks first started to mingle.

Lough Erne is reached via the town of Enniskillen, which was built at the junction of lower and upper Lough Erne. Roads run north around the east and west sides of the Lower Lough, and just north of Enniskillen, on a tiny islet at the foot of this lough, is a good example of a round tower (the function of these buildings was explained in the previous chapter).

The Sheela-na-gig is another very early Irish carving but with a wider general distribution. These stone carvings portray a small female figure with an enlarged vagina, and examples exist as late as medieval times, incorporated into churches as gargoyles in Ireland and elsewhere. The origins of the Sheela-na-gig go back into the mists of Irish prehistory: the figure represents the Irish goddess of creation and may be seen as a natural image of a goddess-orientated society. The Sheela-na-gig has parallels in other earth-centred cultures, such as the American Indian.

There are also a few finely carved 'male' stones from the first millennium BC in Ireland. Said by some to be phallic symbols, they are decorated with fine curvilinear shapes akin to the La Tène metalwork designs. The finest example is the Turoe Stone, found at Turoe, County Galway. Two other examples of this style of Celtic carving can be seen at Mullaghmast, County Kildare, and Castle Strange, County Roscommon.

A stele or pillar at Cardonagh, County Donegal, Ireland, depicting two pilgrim figures. Eighth century AD.

'The Silent Mover'.

Beautiful Books
The Illuminated Gospels

SINCE THEIR creation in the seventh and eighth centuries AD, the great Gospels have provided inspiration for artists and craftspeople throughout the western hemisphere. The designs on many of the finest Celtic crosses, as well as much of the exquisite Celtic metalwork from the sixth to the ninth centuries AD, were created by artists familiar with either the Gospels themselves or the complex geometric principles involved in creating their elaborate designs.

The best known of the great Gospels is the Book of Kells, yet there are a number of lesser-known manuscripts of a similar but slightly later date which were produced throughout Europe under the influence of the Irish monks. One example exists in the library of St Petersburg in Russia, dating from the late eighth century AD. The three Gospels we will examine in this chapter are the Books of Kells, Lindisfarne and Durrow.

The Book of Kells dates from the eighth century AD and takes its name from the early Irish monastic community at Kells, County Meath. It is thought that the book was designed on the island of Iona and, during one of the frequent Viking invasions, taken for safekeeping to this monastery. In the *Annals of Ulster*, dated 1006, it is recorded as having been stolen from the church and found 'after twenty nights and two months, its gold having been stolen off it, and a sod over it'.

The manuscript itself is certainly the wonder of the Celtic world in its beauty and complexity. Many brightly coloured natural pigments are used, blue, green, yellow and red-brown being predominant. The blue was made from finely powdered lapis lazuli, which must have been brought from the Continent as there are no known sources of this mineral in the British Isles.

The ornament in the Book of Kells is most profuse and varied, incorporating in places subtle influences from Pictish and Byzantine art. Spirals, knotwork and chevron or key-patterning, the three main components of Celtic art, are here found at their very best, and the scale of many of the designs is minute. As an example, on the 'Chi-Rho monogram' page there is a panel illustrating four monks pulling each other's beards, and incorporating knotwork designs as well. This panel is only $\frac{9}{10}$ inch (2 cm) wide! It is not fully understood how these motifs were drawn on such a scale, and some method of enlargement or magnification must have been used to paint, say, several bird or plant motifs surrounded by very complex knotwork within the space of a square inch of vellum. The book has been referred to by some as 'the work of angels' and is one of the world's greatest art treasures.

During the Cromwellian period, it was presented to Trinity College, Dublin, probably by Henry Jones, Bishop of Meath from 1661 to 1682. To this day it can still be admired under glass in the library of Trinity College, about 1,200 years after its creation by the early Celtic monks.

A facsimile of the entire book has been created this century by the artist and historian François Henri.[23] This is a wonderful work in its own right and resembles the original manuscript closely.

Lindisfarne is one of the Farne Islands, which lie 1½ miles (2.5 km) off the coast of Northumbria. Today one can make a pilgrimage to the ruins of the eleventh-century priory, which was built on the site of the original monastery. This first monastery was founded c. AD 635 and the great Lindisfarne Gospels were written and illuminated on the island about 100 years later.

There can be no doubt that the Lindisfarne Gospels are very closely related in style to the Book of Kells. The earliest historical references to their origins lie in the book itself. In the tenth century AD a priest called Aldred, about 250 years after the Gospels had been written, added an Anglo-Saxon translation of the Latin text. On the last page he wrote the following:

Eadfrith, Bishop of the Lindisfarne church, originally wrote this book, for God and Saint Cuthbert and, jointly for all the saints whose relics are in the island. And Ethelwald, Bishop of the Lindisfarne islanders, impressed it on the outside, and covered it as he well knew how. And Billfrith the anchorite forged the ornaments which are on it and on the outside adorned it with gold and gems and with gilded-over silver, pure metal. And Aldred, most unworthy and miserable priest, glossed it in English between the lines with the help of God and Saint Cuthbert.[24]

The link with the Irish tradition of great illuminated manuscripts can be traced to the sacred island of Iona. King Oswald of Northumbria, eager to establish Celtic Christianity in his realm, sent a request to Iona for Irish priests to occupy Lindisfarne. A group of missionaries, led by St Aidan, came from Iona and founded the monastery on Holy Island, as Lindisfarne is known. St Cuthbert, to whom the Gospels are dedicated, was born around the time these Irish priests arrived on the island.

The Gospels themselves are almost as magnificent as the Book of Kells. Again the individual panels are minute. The main pages are of exquisite ornateness, employing, as in the Book of Kells, spirals, knotwork and key-patterning of the most intricate nature, as well as birds, mythical beasts and stylized figures of Christ and the four Evangelists.

At the end of the eighth century AD, Lindisfarne was among the many islands, including Iona, which were invaded and pillaged by the Vikings. Fortunately, the great Gospels survived, and several years later were taken to the mainland for safekeeping, along with the reliquary containing the relics of St Cuthbert. For a short period the Gospels remained at Chester-le-Street, County Durham, which was where the priest Aldred added the Anglo-Saxon translation mentioned above.

At a later date the Gospels were taken to Durham Cathedral, along with the relics of St Cuthbert. They then faded into obscurity for some time, not reappearing until 1567, when the *Vocabulum Saxonicum*, the first dictionary of Anglo-Saxon, was produced, using the priest Aldred's Latin/Anglo-Saxon translation in the Gospels as its main guide. During this time the Gospels are believed to have been kept for safety in the Tower of London's Jewel House, probably due to their lavish gold and jewelled binding.

'Knotwork Beast'.

In the early 1600s they were acquired by Sir Robert Cotton, who possessed a magnificent library of ancient manuscripts. Sir Robert's heirs made over the Cottonian collection to the nation in 1703, and in 1753 it was incorporated into the British Museum as one of its major collections. The magnificent Gospels can still be seen there today.

The state of the binding when it was presented to the British Museum was very poor, so in 1852 Smith-Nicholson of Lincoln's Inn Fields, London, a firm of craftsmen-jewellers, rebound them, using mainly silver and precious stones. The coverwork, which is exceptionally beautiful and ornate, employs only designs found within the eighth-century-AD manuscript.

Another wonderful great illuminated Gospel is the Book of Durrow. This is the earliest surviving example of the great Gospels, and its date of creation is placed around AD 675. Today it rests safely in Trinity College, Dublin, along with the Book of Kells and other early manuscripts. The illumination in the book has a basic 'earthiness' which serves to enhance rather than detract from its beauty. Red and yellow ochre, olive-green and black are the predominant colours used, although there are others used sparingly.

A detail from the Book of Durrow carpet page. Seventh century AD.

The Gospels have 248 pages, many of which are profusely decorated. There are six majestic 'carpet pages' filled entirely with Celtic ornament, and the size of the book is 9½ x 5½ inches (24.5 x 14 cm). The detail of the knot-work and spiral decoration is truly magnificent, especially on the carpet pages. On many of the knotwork borders clever play is made with optical illusion by using three different colours in sequence, adding depth to what would otherwise be a comparatively plain design (though no design in the Book of Durrow could possibly be called plain!).

The symbols of the four Evangelists are very stark and basic, yet retain a great sense of power and beauty. Man, the symbol of St Matthew, with his very striking outline and highly chequered coat, has been given the rather undignified name of a 'walking buckle' by some less appreciative historians. The spiral ornament within the Gospels is one of the finest detail and accuracy, and the artist who created this masterpiece was very highly skilled and experienced with this art form.

The Gospels' place of creation is not known. It takes its name from the monastery in County Meath which was founded by St Columba (d. AD 597).

On the last page of the Gospels there is a later inscription testifying that it was present in Durrow monastery at about the turn of the twelfth century.

Three possibilities have been put forward as to its place of creation. The first is Durrow itself, which would seem quite likely as the designs bear much similarity to Irish metalwork of the period.

The second is Iona, which is also quite feasible as the Irish monks are known to have had a very large library of manuscripts, later pillaged by the Vikings.

The third is the island of Lindisfarne, where it could have been a predecessor to the Lindisfarne Gospels.

Irrespective of the place of its creation, the Book of Durrow is the earliest and one of the most magnificent of the great illuminated Celtic Gospels, surviving for over 1,300 years and now in the care of Trinity College library, where a few reproductions of the main pages are available.

The great illuminated Gospels are one of the cornerstones of today's wide revival of interest in all things Celtic. Many artists and craftspeople base their work around designs found in them, or create new ones using the basic principles rediscovered and laid out by the Scottish artist and writer George Bain, the pioneer of the Celtic art revival in this century.[25]

The 'studio reproduction' of the Book of Kells created by François Henri in the 1970s was already a legend in its own right when the idea of a facsimile was taken almost to its limit in 1990 by a firm called Fine Art Facsimile Publishers of Lucerne, in Switzerland. They produced a facsimile of the Book of Kells limited to 1,480 copies, 740 of which were reserved for English-speaking countries. Parchment identical to the original was used, and each page was cut to the size of the corresponding original page. Up to ten colour pigments, which were totally matched with the colours in the original version, were used. Each copy was hand-stitched and hand-bound, using white leather of a variety identical to the original Gospels. The price was original too, being US$14,800 for a pre-publication edition! This magnificent volume has found its way to several special places worldwide where it can be admired and appreciated. Without extremely close scrutiny, it is not possible to distinguish it from the original work. One of the places where a copy can be seen is the abbey on the island of Iona, western Scotland.

An illuminated initial from the Book of Kells. Eighth century AD.

Stone carving of a nobleman in battle-dress, from Iona, western Scotland. Thirteenth century AD.

Columba's Isle
Iona Past and Present

IT SEEMS FITTING to dedicate a complete chapter of this book to a specific place which has had Celtic connections from its earliest recorded history right through to the present day. One of the best examples is the holy island of Iona, off the west coast of Scotland.

The island is located in the Inner Hebrides, about ½ mile (1 km) from the south-west coast of the Isle of Mull and separated from the latter by a stretch of water known as the Sound of Iona. This magical place presents an ever-changing face. In winter it receives the full force of the Atlantic gales and as a consequence there are no trees here whatsoever. Yet on a calm summer's day the sea is an iridescent blue, comparable to the Aegean, due to the fine white sand beneath it.

The author speaks from direct experience, as he has stayed on the island on several occasions, including six winter months in the abbey buildings at a time when the late Dr George MacLeod was still actively coordinating the present Iona Community.

The island has its roots in the dim and distant past, and was almost certainly regarded as a sacred place in prehistoric times. It is known that before the time of St Columba there was a druidic school on the island, and, according to one source,[26] at the time of his arrival the resident archdruid was a Welshman by the name of Gwendollau, with a fellow druid called Myrddin. It has been suggested that this could have been the Merlin of Arthurian legend, but there is no evidence to substantiate this.

One of the early recorded Gaelic names of Iona is 'Innis na druineach' or island of druids, an indication of its importance in pre-Christian times.

One interesting fact relating to druidic times is that the present Coronation stone in Westminster Abbey began its life as the Black Stone of Destiny on Iona. It is said to have been used by the druids, as well as St Columba. The latter is reputed to have crowned King Aedan on the stone. In later years the stone was removed to Scone, where it was reverentially used for the crowning of Scottish monarchs. From there it was removed in the year 1296 to Westminster Abbey, its present resting place, where it has been used for Coronation ceremonies from that date onwards.

This connection of Iona with royalty is seen in better perspective when Columba's life is examined. After launching several missionary journeys to the Scottish mainland, Columba became the spiritual adviser to King Aedan, whose realm extended from the Orkney Isles to the Isle of Man and certain areas of Ireland. Aedan himself was of Irish descent. This role of adviser was a continuation of the druidic tradition of a regional ruler having his or her priest/seer as their oracle. (There is an interesting analogy here with another remote part of the world, Tibet, where a state oracle in the form of a highly trained priest was still employed there until the Chinese occupation of the country in the 1950s.)

Much of the information we have about Iona and St Columba was written by Adamnan, a Celtic monk living on the island in the late seventh century AD. It should be borne in mind that his *Life of St Columba* was written about 100 years after Columba's death, and so may contain a few elaborations and discrepancies.

In the book there are a number of instances relating to the saint's powers of prophecy and clairvoyance, as well as his ability to see and communicate with angels and beings from different realms. Likewise, his ability as a healer was well known. It is written that he possessed a white stone (presumably a quartz pebble) which he had found in a river. This he blessed and used for healing purposes. The latter story gives some insight into the origins of crystal healing, which is widely used today. There is also a custom relating to this which was observed by the Iona fishermen until early this century. Each person would take a pebble of green and white Iona marble with them on fishing trips in these hazardous waters. The pebbles were said to invoke the protection of St Columba and were known as 'Columba's stones'.

One further remarkable story of Columba's travels related in Adamnan's book concerns his encounter with 'Nessie', the Loch Ness monster. It is written that on his missionary travels in the land of the Picts he arrived at a burial taking place beside the loch of a person who had been bitten by a monster from the deep, dark waters. One of Columba's monks swam across the loch to retrieve a boat from the other side and was himself approached by the fearsome monster. Columba raised his hand, making the sign of the cross, and ordered the monster to depart, at which point it vanished again into the depths. Today's 'Nessie' enthusiasts take heart and keep looking!

Returning to Iona itself, a brief tour of the main sites connected with St Columba should prove interesting. A number of these sites would have been used in some form or other prior to this landing on the island in AD 563.

Opposite: *'Columba'*.

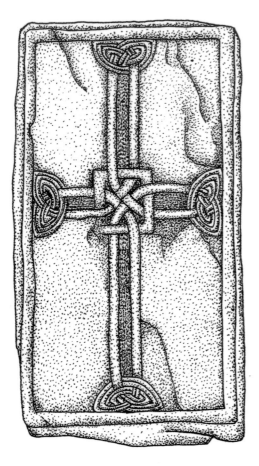

An early Celtic slab cross from Iona, western Scotland. Seventh to eighth century AD.

The abbey church of St Mary is the focal point of the island. It was built on the site of the original monastic settlement of St Columba in the sixth century AD. Much of the building dates from the early thirteenth century, though some parts, as well as individual carved stones, are considerably earlier. The original church was said to have been surrounded by seven small 'satellite' chapels, and the remains of two still exist, as does a small building close to a tiny stream which was said to have been the monk's bakery. Wheat was imported from the nearby island of Tiree, which, despite its northerly location, is very fertile in places and has more sunshine than many other areas of the British Isles.

St Oran's Chapel, mentioned earlier in this book, is of a very early date and stands apart from the abbey buildings. The abbey fell into disrepair at the time of the Dissolution of the Monasteries by Henry VIII, although pilgrimages to the holy island continued to be made by many over the following centuries. The author has a steel engraving of the ruined abbey buildings dated 1772, where the island is referred to as Jona, not Iona. In this highly detailed work there are three deer in the foreground. Certainly none exists on the island today and it would be interesting to know whether this was just artistic licence or, more likely, there actually were deer on the island at that time.

Close to the abbey buildings are the ruins of the nunnery, built in 1203 by Somarlide, Lord of the Isles, when the island came into his possession. Today the grounds have been beautifully laid out as a garden sanctuary. In the vicinity of the abbey buildings are the fine Celtic crosses of St Martin and St John (the latter is a cast of the original, which was taken to the mainland in the 1960s for restoration). Further down the small road to the abbey stands MacLean's cross, also mentioned earlier.

Close to St Oran's Chapel is the Reilig Odhrain, nowadays known as the Burial Ground of the Kings. Being the original home of the Black Stone of

Destiny, later known as the Stone of Scone, it is hardly surprising that Iona had many royal links. Scottish, Irish, Norse and French monarchs and noblemen were buried here from very early times. Some of the most elaborate gravestones, including two Norse ones, are preserved in the island's museum. Such was the sanctity of the island that it was considered the highest privilege to be buried here. This tradition continues to the present day. A recent example is the burial on the island in 1994 of John Smith, leader of the Labour Party, who had a deep love of western Scotland and especially Iona.

The island itself is only 3½ miles (5.5 km) long and 1½ miles (2.5 km) across, and the highest point, Dun I, is just 322 feet (100 m). Due to the flat ground surrounding this granite hill, it looks considerably higher. 'I' (or sometimes Hy) was another early name for the island itself, thus Dun I means 'the hill of Iona'. On the very top of this mound there is a holy well known as the Well of Healing, in which some remarkable cures are said to have taken place. Standing on top of the hill on a clear day and looking at the wondrous view of the Treshnish Islands, the mountains of Mull, Erraid Island and, in the distance, Staffa is in itself a potent healing experience.

Near the south-west foot of Dun I lie the remains of St Columba's beehive cell, mentioned earlier. Travelling clockwise (or rather sun-wise) around the rugged coastline of the island, we come to the marble quarry, near the south-east end of the island. This quarry has been in use in a small way for centuries, small pieces of the beautiful green and white stone being carved into artefacts by pilgrims, to be blessed in the abbey before their return. Around the turn of this century machinery was introduced to excavate more marble for supplying the ever-increasing visitors to the island with polished artefacts. Fortunately, due to a combination of Atlantic

A burial slab with foliate style decoration and Celtic ornament, Iona, western Scotland. Thirteenth century AD.

weather and inaccessibility, this operation soon ceased and the only evidence of its existence is a gaunt and very rusted mechanical hoist still *in situ* at the quarry. For the devout pilgrims of yesterday and today, wonderful examples of Iona marble pebbles can be found on some of the remote beaches of the island, smoothed and polished by nature's master of crafts, the sea.

At the most southerly point of the island lies Columba's Bay. It was here that he landed with his twelve followers. He is said to have walked inland to a raised mound and, surveying the horizon from this point, found that Ireland was no longer visible. The king of Ireland's command fulfilled, he and his monks decided to settle on the island.

A local folk-custom still exists whereby persons wishing to rid themselves of any unwanted or outmoded thought patterns will make a pilgrimage to this remote beach. Picking up a stone from the shoreline, a prayer is said and the stone is then flung into the sea. The act symbolizes the casting away of unwanted thoughts.

Columba's Bay has an unrestricted view to the south and on a clear day the visibility can be as much as 40 miles (70 km). Thus the higher ground above it would have made an ideal lookout for 'visitors' both welcome and unwelcome, and would almost certainly have been used as such even before Columba's time.

On the western side of the island is a beautiful beach of white sand called the Machair. From this point the islands of Tiree and Coll are clearly visible. Iona is said to have had its own school of stonemasons who carved Celtic crosses and elaborate slab stones. A number of the crosses were commissioned for other parts of western Scotland, and it is thought that the finished carvings were loaded on to boats from this sandy beach. The Kildalton cross on the island of Islay and the Campbeltown cross are examples of early and late crosses which are said to have been carved on Iona. The Kildalton cross dates from the eighth century AD and the Campbeltown cross from the fourteenth. As the Campbeltown cross was one of the last Celtic crosses to be carved in western Scotland, this gives a time-span of some 600 years of high-quality Celtic stone-carving on the island, which is quite remarkable!

Inland from the Machair is a small hillock known as the Hill of the Angels. It is said that here St Columba saw and conversed with angels. This story has many similarities with visions of the *sidhe* in the Irish sagas, which describe events of an earlier era. Until the beginning of this century it was the local custom on the Feast of St Michael, 29 September, to celebrate this day by walking sun-wise around the Hill of the Angels. The Feast of St

Michael was one of the great events of the year in the Western Isles until the middle of the nineteenth century.[27] He was known in Gaelic as 'cra-gheal', literally 'red-white', symbolizing the red of courage and the white purity of spirit.

We end our sun-wise tour of the island at its northern end, where there is another beach of white sand known as the White Strand of the Monks. Past events here were not so savoury, as the monks connected with this beautiful beach were massacred by the Vikings during one of their fierce raids on the island. Standing on this beach today, there is a fine view on a clear day of Ben More, the highest mountain on the Isle of Mull, which rises to over 3,500 feet (1,080 m).

Across the Sound of Iona, near the village of Fionnphort, the medieval ruins of several small pilgrims' houses are still visible. Having travelled the ancient route across the Isle of Mull, pilgrims could shelter here for the night, before crossing the water to the holy island. Nearby is Pennyghael, where at one time the Iona monks cultivated a herb garden.

The present-day Celtic Community on the island was started by pioneering work of one man, the Reverend Dr George MacLeod, who passed on into Higher Dimensions in 1991 at the grand age of ninety-six.

To have a vision of a goal is one thing, but to achieve that goal often seems to be too daunting a task. Many brilliant ideas have 'vapourized' due to an inability to ground them and bring them fully into being.

Fortunately, this was far from the case with Dr MacLeod and the Iona Community. In the 1930s he was parish minister of Govan, one of the most deprived areas of Glasgow. He became increasingly disillusioned with the apathy of the conventional Church and its attitude to the plight of working-class communities and the unemployed. In 1938, despite having a very well-attended church with crowded services, he resigned.

Along with six ministers and six lay workers, he then set out to rebuild the ruins of the Iona abbey buildings, which had been derelict since Henry VIII's Dissolution of the Monasteries. The whole essence of the story of this remarkable man has strong parallels with that of St Columba, who also left Ireland with twelve followers to create an enlightened community on Iona.

The author recalls an occasion in the 1960s, crossing the Sound of Iona with Dr MacLeod in the small ferry during a force eight gale. The few passengers not being sick were clutching on to the sides of the craft very apprehensively. However, Dr MacLeod was standing upright in the stern of the boat, completely soaked by the spray, the wind almost tearing the cloak from his back. One hand was outstretched and he was thanking God for this wonderful display of weather! That image, in conjunction with thoughts about reincarnation, evoked a picture in the author's mind of a possible 'returned' Celtic saint. Definitely a 'man with a mission'!

Slowly and patiently, the rebuilding of the abbey buildings continued over the years, and as word spread the project attracted workers first from Scotland's cities and later from all parts of the world.

Many so-called 'coincidental' events occurred. For example, during the Second World War, there was a shortage of timber for the dormitory roof. Timber on the island is non-existent and even then was extremely expensive to buy and transport from the mainland. Very shortly after this an entire cargo of wood drifted on to one of the nearby beaches and was found to be exactly the right size for the required job.

As a tribute to this great man's perseverance and vision, the abbey buildings were finally completed in 1967, almost thirty years after the work had begun. Considering the extreme remoteness of this tiny island, and also the intervention of the war from 1939 to 1945, the completion of this project was nothing short of miraculous. The author writes about the Community from firsthand experience as he participated in the project over the winter of 1964. By this time the major constructional work had been completed.

The ideals of the present-day community, when seen from a historical and spiritual perspective, are an organic evolution of St Columba's original Celtic community on the island in the sixth century AD. These ideals of Celtic Christianity are like a breath of fresh air to the staid and dogmatic 'Churchianity' which still exists in many places today. The fact is that the Iona Community in the 1990s attracts many contemporary pilgrims of all ages and beliefs and from all parts of the world. Their schedules are always fully booked, which is a testament to the rapidly growing living spirit of the Celtic Christian way of life. This is seen by many as the vehicle by which Christianity, rather than declining even further, can be carried forward into the twenty-first century within an ecological and practical framework whose basis consists of a joyful, natural, spirit-filled and planetary-aware way of life.

The present-day community has around 200 full members, mainly in Britain but also in Africa, New Zealand, India, Europe, Australia, Canada and America – shades of the travelling monks described earlier in this book! Among the many commitments of the community are dedication to the poor and the exploited, both in Britain and abroad; dedication to action in the areas of justice and peacemaking, both among societies and nations, and in relation to the earth; commitment to interfaith meetings, and action about racism; commitment to finding new ways of worship (they have already initiated some most inspiring nature-orientated seasonal services, in harmony with the Celtic way); commitment to healing; and commitment to the concerns of young people. The community has its own publishing arm, Wild Goose Publications,[28] which produces books, cassettes and a regular publication, *The Coracle*.

The restored abbey welcomes up to fifty guests each week from all over the world, as well as many thousands of pilgrims during the summer months. An extension of the community buildings, the MacLeod Centre, founded on Dr MacLeod's nintieth birthday in 1985, also houses up to fifty guests of all ages, backgrounds and traditions, and has been built with a crafts room and adapted facilities for those with mobility difficulties. It is certainly a place that St Columba would have endorsed and actively participated in, and no doubt still does on some level!

The community also runs the Camas outdoor centre on Mull, which is possibly the nearest younger people will get to the satisfying and basic Celtic lifestyle. The emphasis here is on the outdoors and closeness to nature. The buildings were originally a salmon-fishing station and are on the edge of Camas Bay, accessible only by a twenty-minute walk over the moor after you reach the road's end. Work and worship are at the heart of Camas, and the centre is orientated towards young people from urban backgrounds. Sensibly, the staff have decided not to install electricity, so activities here are carried out according to the sun (or lack of it) and the seasons. Camas provides a 'once in a lifetime' experience for many young and adventurous folk.

A fitting conclusion to this chapter on Iona, the Mecca of the Gael, would be words Dr MacLeod himself once used to describe the island: 'It is a "thin place" – where only tissue paper separates the material from the spiritual.'

To be there is to experience this.

Celtic Renaissance
The Continuing Tradition

THOUGH THERE has been steady but quietly unbroken continuity of the Celtic art form in all the Celtic countries, especially Ireland and Wales, it is really only since the turn of this century that the Celtic art revival has proceeded with vigour. Today in the 1990s it is ever on the increase.

One of the first pioneers of this revival was the artist, writer and historian J. Romilly Allen. This dedicated man visited, sketched and researched many Celtic sites and carvings in the British Isles and Europe, especially those in Scotland, Ireland and Wales. After several years of work, he published a book, *Celtic Art in Pagan and Christian Times*, in 1904. The book put forward new theories as to the origins of Celtic art, many of which have subsequently been proved correct. It was also the first comprehensive treatise on the art-work of the Celtic countries, listing and categorizing sites and carvings.

Following on from Romilly Allen's work several decades later, George Bain, the man who more than anyone to date has fostered and promoted the re-emergence of the Celtic art form, began his work. Initially he produced several small books, which were used in Scottish schools to encourage and revive this beautiful art form. His painstaking work involved the first redis-covery of the actual methods of construction of the Celtic patterns since their inception during the seventh century AD or even earlier. He based his research around not only the great illuminated Gospels of Kells and Lindisfarne but also lesser-known works such as the Gospels of MacRegol and the Book of Armagh. His tireless dedication eventually produced one comprehensive book, which has been used by students of Celtic art world-wide since its publication in 1951. In this book the geometric principles used by the early Celtic monks to create knotwork, spiral and key patterns are carefully explained, enabling the creative artist of today to produce his or her own original designs, starting from the first principles.

Today there are artists and craftspeople working in almost every medium, utilizing Celtic designs. The intrinsic beauty of these patterns is so strong

Opposite: 'Resurrection'. This incorporates St Piran's Cross, Perranporth, Cornwall; ninth century AD.

that it is very easy to see why the art form has become so well loved. There are craftworkers in precious and base metals, ceramics, wood, enamel, stained glass, stone and leather, to name just some of the media used to create Celtic works of great beauty.

In small pockets of the Celtic countries, crafts with some Celtic ornamentation have been produced from Victorian times or even earlier, the artists involved deriving their own inspiration from early manuscripts, and sometimes combining this with further inspiration from figures out of the early Irish sagas, or perhaps the Welsh *Mabinogion*. There are still artists and craftworkers today whose work is solely inspired in this manner, but the majority have gained their initial training from the first principles rediscovered by George Bain. The more creative of these artists then carry on to create totally new and original designs and images based on the ancient geometric principles.

This art form has been developed by enthusiasts not just in the Celtic countries but worldwide. However, some of the finest work is still produced in Ireland, Wales, Scotland, the Isle of Man, Cornwall and Brittany. Remote areas of the Celtic world seem highly conducive to creativity, and there are high-quality crafts being produced in such places as the Outer Hebrides and the Shetland Islands, as well as remote mountainous areas of Wales and islands off the west coast of Ireland. The true Celtic spirit, however, can flourish anywhere, and some equally fine crafts are being produced throughout mainland Britain in both rural and urban locations.

The revival does not stop with arts and crafts. There is a great revival of Celtic music, using original instruments such as the clarsach or Celtic harp; the bodhrán, which is the original Irish hand-drum; Uilleann and Northumbrian pipes, as well as the Scottish bagpipes; the Breton bombarde, open-holed flute and other early instruments. Recently, with the addition of amplified instruments, 'folk-rock' has become widespread and good-quality bands have provided some extremely fine music, blending early instruments with electric guitar, drums and keyboard.

Other Celtic musicians prefer to keep to one single instrument and tastefully produce their own arrangements and adaptations of traditional tunes. There are, for example, a few extremely talented harpists today who, as well as playing their own compositions and traditional airs, have adapted many of the early tunes by the blind Irish harpist Turlough O'Carolan. Born in 1670, the son of a farmer in Newtown, County Meath, O'Carolan was blinded by smallpox at the age of eighteen, but went on to become one of the most famous Irish harpists, leaving a legacy of over 200 pieces of music, many of which survive today.

'St Michael'.

There is also a widespread revival of interest in Celtic languages. This has occurred at a very opportune time, as some were almost on the verge of becoming extinct. Cornish is an example, the language having been researched and recently revived from an almost non-existent state. Happily, there is now a full Cornish dictionary in print and a number of people are involved in both teaching and learning the language. The same revival is under way with the Breton language, although this has continued to be used in rural areas from early times to the present day. The author recalls being introduced in the early 1960s to two elderly ladies living on the island of Sark in the Channel Islands, whose sole language since childhood had been traditional Breton.

Scots Gaelic is enjoying a healthy revival, with centres offering courses and postal tuition. There are several hours of Gaelic television transmissions weekly, and in 1993 the government in Scotland pledged £9 million towards a Gaelic televison fund. There are also excellent Gaelic musicians of various styles giving live performances, and a National Gaelic Mod is held each October.

The Welsh language has continued in an unbroken tradition from early times to the present day, and it is the first language of a large number of people from all walks of life. There is a Welsh television channel, as well as newspapers, periodicals and a continuous flow of new books, music and dramatic productions. The language is also taught in schools and university departments, and the annual Eisteddfod festival is internationally renowned.

Irish is also very much alive and well, enjoying a major revival. In some of the remote parts of western Ireland, it is still used as a first language, but there are now schools, societies and centres where the language is taught and encouraged. The Irish Tourist Board has succeeded in promoting the island's Celtic culture in a realistic fashion, without succumbing to commercialization.

There are magazines devoted to the preservation and continuance of all the Celtic languages; one based on the Isle of Man incorporates individual articles translated into each of the different Celtic languages.[29]

From this chapter it can be seen that the Celtic spirit is vibrant and expanding in many important areas of people's lives. So what is the underlying reason for this Celtic resurgence?

The answer would seem to lie in the fact that today's style of living in the Western world has alienated so many people from their true selves that a way back has become a dire necessity, before a point of no return is reached. One practical and positive path available to help us regain our wholeness is closer attunement to nature, the seasons and all aspects of the natural world. This involves observation of the tides and the lunar phases, the respect and care for Mother Earth, Her trees, water and all Her inhabitants, both human and animal, and seeing the life force or spirit in all things, including ourselves. The creative energy generated by adopting such a way of life can then be used in many different ways, from arts, crafts and music to the mundane tasks of everyday living. However, even everyday living, when seen in this light, becomes a joy rather than a burden, and our whole being will absorb and emit a radiance which will in turn uplift those we meet, whatever our occupation may be.

This, surely, is the true way of the Celtic spirit.

May this book and its images inspire you to discover some of the many joys of this Celtic renaissance.

'St Michael'.

References and
Further Reading

BEFORE GOING to the modern sources, it is worth looking at the works of those classical authors who recorded their experiences of the early Celtic peoples and are mentioned in this book: Ammianus Marcellinus, Dio Cassius, Diodorus Siculus, Julius Caesar, Livy, Pliny the Elder, Polybius, Strabo and Tacitus.

A useful general reference book on the Latin texts is *Latin Selections*, edited by Moses Hadas and Thomas Suits, Dover Publications, New York, 1992.

* 1 *The Sacred Yew: Rediscovering the Ancient Tree of Life through the Work of Allen Meredith,* Anand Cheton and Diana Brueton, Penguin/Arcana, 1994

2 *Sacred Stones, Sacred Places,* Marianna Lines, St Andrews Press, 1993

* 3 *Celtic Art: The Methods of Construction,* George Bain, William MacLellan, 1951 (recent reprint by Dover Publications)

* 4 *The Art of Celtia,* Courtney Davis, Blandford Press, 1993

* 5 *Gerald of Wales: The History and Topography of Ireland,* J. J. O'Meara (ed.), 1982

* 6 *The Work of Angels,* Susan Young (ed.), British Museum Publications, 1990

* 7 *The Manx Crosses Illuminated,* Maureen Costain Richards, Croshag Publications, 1988.

8 'Celtic Coinage', Frank James, *Celtic Connections,* Nos. 7 and 8, 1994

9 'Trees: The Cradle of a Race', Brian Lavelle, *Celtic Connections,* Nos. 10 and 11, 1995

* 10 *The Sacred Yew,* see 1

11 Ibid.

* 12 *Secret Shrines: In Search of the Old Holy Wells of Cornwall,* Paul Broadhurst, Pendragon Press, 1991

* 13 *The Well of the Triple Goddess,* Brian Slade, Sheppey Archaeological Society, Santa Maria Publications, 1994

* 14 *The Fairy Faith in Celtic Countries,* W. Y. Evans Wentz, Colin Smythe Ltd, 1977 (originally published by Oxford University Press, 1911)

* 15 *The Orion Mystery,* Robert Bauval and Adrian Gilbert, Heinemann Press, 1994

16 *The Celtic Druids' Year,* John King, Blandford Press, 1994

* 17 *Sun and Cross,* Jacob Streit, Floris Books, 1993

* 18 *Wisdom of the Celtic Saints,* Edward C. Sellner, Ave Maria Press, USA, 1993

* 19 *The Brendan Voyage,* Tim Severin, Hutchinson, 1978

20 *Sacred Stones, Sacred Places,* see 2

* 21 *Celtic Art in Pagan and Christian Times,* J. Romilly Allen, 1904 (reprinted by Bracken Books, London, 1993

* 22 *The Manx Crosses Illuminated,* see 7

* 23 *The Book of Kells,* studio reproduction by François Henri, Thames and Hudson, *c.* 1974

24 *The Book of Lindisfarne,* Janet Backhouse, Phaidon Press, 1981

* 25 *Celtic Art: The Methods of Construction,* see 3

* 26 *The Western Mystery Tradition,* C. Hartley, Aquarian Press, 1968

* 27 *The Sun Dances: Prayers and Blessings from the Gaelic, Collected in the Highlands and Islands by Dr Alexander Carmichael (1832–1912),* The Christian Community Press, London, 1960

* 28 Wild Goose Publications, The Iona Community, Pearce Institute, Govan, Glasgow G51 3UU, Scotland

* 29 *CARN: Journal of the Celtic League,* Farmhill, Braddan, Isle of Man

* For reference and further reading only; no text quoted from book

Index

Page numbers in *italic* refer to the illustrations